Leadership in the Age of Data: Harnessing Information for Strategic Advantage

Gideon Ikwe

Published by Gideon Ikwe, 2024.

While every precaution has been taken in the preparation of this book, the publisher assumes no responsibility for errors or omissions, or for damages resulting from the use of the information contained herein.

LEADERSHIP IN THE AGE OF DATA: HARNESSING INFORMATION FOR STRATEGIC ADVANTAGE

First edition. March 20, 2024.

Copyright © 2024 Gideon Ikwe.

Written by Gideon Ikwe.

Table of Contents

Leadership in the Age of Data: Harnessing Information for Strategic Advantage 1

The Evolution of Data-Driven Leadership 5

Qualities of a Data-Driven Leader 16

The Data Landscape 28

Data Governance and Ethics 39

Integrating Data Analytics Into Decision Processes 53

Driving Innovation With Data 64

Cultivating a Data-Driven Culture 79

Data-Driven Strategic Planning 92

Building and Leading Data-Driven Teams 105

Emerging Trends and Future Considerations 118

Best Practices for Data-Driven Leadership 130

Introduction

In the labyrinthine corridors of history, where each turn and each doorway leads to pivotal moments that have shaped humanity, there exists a particular juncture that set the stage for the modern era's most transformative force: data. Cast your mind back to the dawn of the 20th century, a period brimming with industrial revolution and technological marvels, where the seeds of today's data-driven world were sown.

Imagine a world where decisions, from the mundane to the monumental, were guided by gut feelings, personal experience, and the occasional advice of a trusted confidante. This was a time when business moguls and political leaders alike relied on intuition and limited empirical evidence to navigate the choppy waters of their respective domains. It was an era before the computer, before the internet, and long before the advent of big data analytics.

However, as the century progressed, key historical milestones began to reshape this landscape. The invention of the computer, followed by the birth of the internet, heralded new possibilities that were previously the stuff of science fiction. These technological leaps, combined with advancements in statistical methods and the exponential growth in data generation, paved the way for the data-rich environment we inhabit today.

From the past to the present, the transformation has been nothing short of revolutionary. The sheer volume of data available at our fingertips and the sophistication of tools to analyze and interpret this data have revolutionized decision-making processes across industries. Today, leaders are faced with the dual challenge and opportunity of navigating this deluge of information, extracting actionable insights, and leveraging them for strategic advantage.

Why does history matter now, you might ask? Because understanding the journey from intuition-based to data-driven decision-making illuminates the critical importance of embracing data in our current era. It underscores the evolution of leadership and strategy in the face of technological advancements and highlights the potential pitfalls of ignoring this invaluable resource.

As we delve into the contemporary exploration of Leadership in the Age of Data: Harnessing Information for Strategic Advantage, we embark on a journey to dissect the essence of modern leadership in a world awash with data.

The era of data-driven decision-making has dawned, marking a definitive shift from the historical reliance on intuition. This transformation is vividly illustrated by contrasting the decision-making processes of yesteryears, grounded in intuition and limited empirical evidence, with today's methods that employ statistical analysis, predictive modeling, and real-time insights. These advanced techniques not only enhance the accuracy, efficiency, and innovation of strategic decisions but also provide leaders with a tangible competitive edge.

INDICE

INTRODUZIONE 2024	3
NOTA INTRODUTTIVA	5
IL DOLORE – CENNI STORICI	15
Premessa	15
La concezione del dolore nei tempi remoti. I precursori della neurofisiologia e degli antidolorifici.	23
Il dolore nelle grandi religioni	57
Il Medioevo	101
L'età moderna	107
L'anestesia generale	117
L'anestesia locale	129
Le acquisizioni recenti: Il problema della specificità nei nocicettori La "teoria del cancello" di Ronald Melzack	135
La misurazione del dolore	145
APPENDICI	153
CRONOLOGIE	155
- NEUROLOGIA	155
- ANESTESIA E ANTALGIA	159

IL DIBATTITO CONTEMPORANEO SU GIOBBE 165

La prospettiva scientifica. 165
La prospettiva metafisica: il dolore dell'innocente. 170
La prospettiva metafisica: la sofferenza di Dio. 176
Auschwitz. 183

BIBLIOGRAFIA 191

LEADERSHIP IN THE AGE OF DATA: HARNESSING INFORMATION FOR STRATEGIC ADVANTAGE

Leaders are now compelled to not just acknowledge but actively embrace the integration of data and analytics into their leadership style and organizational culture. The exponential growth in data availability, paired with the sophistication of analytical tools, presents a unique set of challenges and opportunities. Embracing a data-centric approach can unveil hidden opportunities, mitigate risks, and tailor offerings to meet precise market demands, highlighting the imperative for leaders to adapt.

This book serves as a roadmap, guiding you through the evolution of data-driven leadership, the essential qualities of a data-savvy leader, and practical strategies for embedding data-driven practices within organizations. Each chapter is designed to demystify the concept of data-driven leadership, provide actionable strategies for harnessing data in leadership tasks, and inspire a cultural shift towards data-centric thinking within organizations.

Our journey will equip leaders with the mindset, skills, and knowledge necessary to thrive in an era where data represents a pivotal asset for success. Through a blend of historical insights, contemporary examples, and future-looking perspectives, "Leadership in the Age of Data" asserts that the ability to harness data for strategic advantage is not merely an option but a defining characteristic of successful leaders and organizations in the modern era.

As we turn the page to the next chapter, remember this: embracing the data revolution is not just about surviving in the ever-evolving business landscape—it's about thriving. Leaders who dare to embrace the transformative power of data will not only navigate the complexities of the modern world more effectively but will also steer their organizations toward unprecedented success.

Are you ready to embrace the data revolution and lead your organization into a new era of strategic advantage?

The Evolution of Data-Driven Leadership

Historical Perspective on Leadership and Data Usage

In the annals of history, the utilization of data for leadership and decision-making has undergone a metamorphosis, evolving from rudimentary methods to sophisticated, data-driven strategies that define the contemporary era. This journey, marked by key inflection points, underscores the transformative role of data in shaping strategic advantage.

Long before the term 'data' entered the lexicon of leaders, ancient civilizations demonstrated an intuitive grasp of its underlying principles. The Egyptians meticulously calculated the flooding patterns of the Nile to optimize agricultural yields, an early testament to leveraging environmental data for societal benefit. Similarly, the builders of the Roman Empire employed surveys and land registers to administer vast territories, effectively using data to maintain control and facilitate governance. These examples, though primitive by today's standards, illustrate a foundational understanding of data's utility in guiding decisions.

The dawn of the Renaissance heralded a shift towards more systematic approaches to data collection and analysis. Astronomers like Copernicus and Galileo challenged prevailing wisdom through meticulous observations, essentially relying on empirical data to advance human understanding of the universe. Their work exemplified the burgeoning recognition of data's potential to unravel complexities and yield insights.

However, it was during the Industrial Revolution that data began to assert its significance in optimizing production and enhancing efficiency. The advent of statistical methods and mechanical tabulating machines allowed businesses to process information with unprecedented speed and accuracy. Factory owners and managers started to track production metrics, labor efficiency, and inventory levels, transforming raw data into actionable insights that drove operational improvements and competitive advantage.

What then, catalyzed the leap from mechanical processing to the digital age, characterized by an explosion of data?

The introduction of computers marked this critical inflection point. Initially, their adoption was limited to government and large corporations due to their prohibitive costs and complexity. Yet, as technology advanced, computers became more accessible, revolutionizing the way data was collected, stored, and analyzed. This digital revolution laid the groundwork for the next quantum leap: the advent of the internet.

The internet's emergence transformed data from a scarce resource to an omnipresent flood, accessible to leaders and organizations worldwide. Information on market trends, consumer behaviors, and competitive strategies became available in real-time, providing a wealth of data that, if harnessed effectively, could offer significant strategic advantage.

Imagine the stark contrast between a 19th-century factory owner poring over production logs and a modern-day executive analyzing real-time data streams from across the globe. The scale and scope of data have expanded exponentially, presenting both opportunities and challenges for today's leaders.

The digital age has not only increased access to data but also the means to analyze it. The development of sophisticated analytics software and artificial intelligence has enabled leaders to uncover patterns, predict trends, and make informed decisions with a level of precision unimaginable in previous eras. Data analytics has become a cornerstone of strategic planning, offering insights that can be the difference between success and obsolescence.

Yet, the abundance of data also poses a significant challenge: the risk of becoming overwhelmed by information, unable to discern what is relevant and actionable. The skillful leader in the age of data is not merely one who has access to information but one who can judiciously sift through the noise, identifying and leveraging data that aligns with strategic objectives.

Consider the implications of this evolution for leadership. The transition from intuition-based to data-driven decision-making signifies a profound change in how leaders approach problems, develop strategies, and steer their organizations. It demands a new set of competencies, including a deep understanding of data analytics, the ability to integrate technological tools, and the foresight to anticipate how data trends will shape the future.

In reflecting on this historical journey, one cannot help but wonder: What lies ahead in the trajectory of leadership and data usage? As we stand on the brink of advancements such as quantum computing and the further proliferation of the internet of things, the potential for data to inform and guide leadership decisions will only magnify.

The leaders who will thrive in this evolving landscape are those who recognize the power of data to unlock insights, drive innovation, and create sustainable competitive advantage. They will be the ones who not only adapt to the age of data but who also lead the charge in harnessing its potential.

As we navigate the complexities of the digital age, let us draw inspiration from the leaders of the past who, in their own times, understood the value of data. Let their journey remind us that at the heart of strategic advantage lies the ability to turn information into insight, and insight into action.

The age of data-driven leadership is upon us. Are we ready to embrace its challenges and opportunities?

Transition From Gut-Feeling Decisions to Data-Driven Strategies

In the wake of this historical evolution toward data-driven leadership, a critical question emerges: How have leaders and organizations bridged the chasm between traditional intuition-based decision-making and the contemporary reliance on data analytics? This transition, neither swift nor uniform across industries, illuminates the cultural and technological transformations that have compelled leaders to adopt a more empirical approach to strategy.

Embarking on this exploration, it becomes evident that the shift to data-driven strategies didn't occur in a vacuum. A confluence of factors—ranging from technological advancements to changing market dynamics—has reshaped the landscape of leadership decision-making.

Initially, the resistance to abandoning gut-feeling decisions was palpable. Many seasoned leaders, steeped in years of experience, viewed the reliance on data with skepticism, if not outright disdain. They prided themselves on their ability to read situations, people, and markets based on intuition honed over decades. Yet, the relentless pace of technological change and the increasingly complex global market environment began to erode the foundations of this intuition-based approach.

Technological advancements, particularly in data collection and analytics software, have significantly lowered the barriers to adopting data-driven strategies. Suddenly, leaders found themselves with access to tools that could sift through vast amounts of information, identify patterns, and predict outcomes with a level of precision previously unimaginable. This technological leap forward provided the impetus for a cultural shift within organizations, as the value of data-driven decision-making became increasingly apparent.

Consider the case of a mid-sized retail chain that embarked on this transition. Previously, decisions regarding inventory, marketing strategies, and store locations were made based on the leadership team's collective experience and market observations. This approach, while successful in a more stable market environment, began to falter as consumer preferences shifted rapidly and online competition intensified.

The turning point came when the company decided to integrate data analytics into its decision-making processes. By analyzing customer data, market trends, and supply chain dynamics, the retail chain could make more informed decisions regarding inventory management and marketing strategies. The results were transformative. Inventory turnover improved, marketing campaigns became more targeted and effective, and overall, the company saw a significant uptick in profitability and market share.

This before-and-after scenario underscores the impact of transitioning to a data-driven strategy. The key to success lay not just in adopting new technologies but in fostering a culture that values data and empirical evidence over intuition and tradition.

Another poignant example comes from the manufacturing sector. A manufacturing company, traditionally run by a family with a strong emphasis on "the way we've always done things," found itself struggling to keep up with competitors who were leveraging data analytics to optimize their production processes and supply chains. The company's leadership, recognizing the need for change, embarked on a comprehensive data analytics program. They started with small, manageable projects to build confidence and demonstrate quick wins, such as optimizing energy consumption and reducing waste on the production floor.

The results spoke volumes. Production efficiency saw a marked improvement, costs were significantly reduced, and the company was able to respond more agilely to market demand changes. This shift not only bolstered the company's competitive position but also changed the internal conversation around decision-making. Data-driven strategies became the new norm, a testament to the cultural shift that had occurred within the organization.

These case studies highlight the transformative power of embracing data-driven strategies. The transition from gut-feeling decisions to data analytics is not merely a change in tools or processes but a fundamental shift in mindset. Leaders must be willing to challenge their assumptions, question the status quo, and embrace the uncertainties that come with interpreting data.

So, what does this transition imply for the future of leadership? It suggests that the leaders who will excel in the age of data are those who can blend the art of leadership with the science of data analytics. They will be the ones who recognize that data, while an invaluable asset, is not a panacea. The most effective leaders will be those who can harness the power of data while also leveraging their intuition and experience to interpret and act on that data in a way that aligns with their organization's strategic objectives.

In conclusion, the journey from gut-feeling decisions to data-driven strategies is marked by both challenges and opportunities. As we look toward the future, it is clear that data will continue to play a pivotal role in shaping strategic decisions. However, the essence of leadership in the age of data lies in the ability to navigate the interplay between empirical evidence and human judgment. This balance will define the strategic advantage in the increasingly complex and data-driven business landscape.

The age of data-driven leadership is not just upon us; it is evolving, compelling leaders to adapt, innovate, and envision new possibilities for the future. Are you ready to lead in this new era?

The Impact of Big Data and Analytics on Leadership Practices

The Evolution of Data-Driven Leadership

In this chapter, we delve into the historical evolution of data-driven leadership and the pivotal role played by big data and analytics in shaping contemporary leadership practices. The transition from traditional intuition-based decision-making to the integration of data analytics has not only transformed the way leaders approach strategic decision-making but has also redefined the skill sets and competencies required for effective leadership in the age of data.

The Advent of Big Data and Analytics

LEADERSHIP IN THE AGE OF DATA: HARNESSING INFORMATION FOR STRATEGIC ADVANTAGE

The era of big data has ushered in an unprecedented influx of information, presenting both challenges and opportunities for leaders across various industries. The exponential growth in data volume, velocity, and variety has necessitated a paradigm shift in leadership practices. Organizations are now grappling with the task of harnessing this abundance of data to derive actionable insights that can drive strategic advantage.

The convergence of sophisticated analytics, machine learning, and artificial intelligence has enabled leaders to parse through vast datasets, identify patterns, and make predictions with unparalleled precision. These technologies have not only augmented the decision-making capabilities of leaders but have also empowered them to anticipate market trends, consumer behavior, and competitive dynamics with a level of accuracy previously unattainable.

Challenges and Opportunities

The transition to data-driven leadership is not without its challenges. Leaders are confronted with the need to acquire new skills and competencies to effectively leverage data analytics in their decision-making processes. The ability to interpret complex data sets, understand statistical methodologies, and communicate data-driven insights to diverse stakeholders has become imperative for leaders navigating the age of data.

Moreover, ethical considerations loom large in the realm of data-driven leadership. The responsible collection, storage, and utilization of data necessitate a heightened awareness of privacy concerns, data security, and the ethical implications of leveraging personal and organizational data for decision-making purposes. Leaders are thus tasked with establishing robust ethical frameworks and governance structures to ensure the ethical and responsible use of data in their strategic endeavors.

However, amidst these challenges, the age of big data and analytics presents a myriad of opportunities for leaders to drive innovation and strategic pivoting. The transformative insights derived from data analytics have the potential to revolutionize business models, optimize operational processes, and unlock new avenues for growth and expansion. Leaders who adeptly harness the power of data are poised to gain a competitive edge in an increasingly data-centric business landscape.

The Cultural Shift in Leadership Decision-Making

The integration of data analytics into leadership practices represents a profound cultural shift within organizations. The historical resistance to relinquishing intuition-based decision-making in favor of empirical evidence has given way to a recognition of the intrinsic value of data-driven strategies. This cultural transformation is underpinned by the realization that data analytics not only augment decision-making processes but also foster a culture of evidence-based reasoning and strategic foresight.

Case studies from diverse industries underscore the transformative power of embracing data-driven strategies. Organizations that have successfully integrated data analytics

LEADERSHIP IN THE AGE OF DATA: HARNESSING INFORMATION FOR STRATEGIC ADVANTAGE

into their decision-making processes have witnessed tangible improvements in operational efficiency, marketing effectiveness, and overall profitability. These success stories serve as compelling testaments to the pivotal role of data-driven leadership in driving organizational success in the age of data.

In the subsequent chapters, we will delve deeper into the intricacies of data-driven leadership, exploring the nuances of implementing data analytics in diverse organizational contexts, and elucidating the competencies and capabilities essential for leaders to navigate the complexities of the data-driven business landscape. The age of data heralds a new era of leadership, one where the fusion of empirical evidence and strategic acumen is paramount in shaping the future trajectory of organizations.

Qualities of a Data-Driven Leader

Analytical Mindset and Data Literacy

In an era where data flows like the rivers that carved the Earth's surface, leaders must navigate these torrents with precision and insight. The compass guiding this journey? An analytical mindset paired with data literacy. These are not mere buzzwords but the bedrock of strategic advantage in the modern age.

At the heart of an analytical mindset lies an insatiable curiosity. Picture a child, eyes wide with wonder, questioning the workings of the world. This same curiosity fuels leaders, driving them to ask, "Why?" and "What if?" at every turn. It's this relentless inquiry that uncovers the true story behind the numbers.

But curiosity alone isn't enough. Like a detective piecing together clues from disparate sources, leaders must possess statistical competence. Imagine staring at a sea of data points, each a star in the night sky. Without the knowledge to connect these dots, they remain just that—dots. Statistical competence is the ability to discern patterns, to see constellations among stars.

Critical thinking is the third pillar, the skill that allows leaders to not just take data at face value but to probe deeper. "Is this the whole story?" "What's missing?" It's like examining a painting, noticing not just the broad strokes but also the subtle nuances hidden in the shadows. This level of scrutiny ensures decisions are not just data-driven, but wisdom-guided.

So, how does one cultivate these skills, both in oneself and within a team? The journey begins with education. Not the dry, lecture-heavy education of yesteryears, but a vibrant, interactive learning experience. Workshops that simulate real-world scenarios, online courses that can be accessed anytime, anywhere—these are the tools that sharpen the mind and foster data literacy.

Hands-on experience, though, is where theory meets reality. Consider a musician learning a new piece; there's a world of difference between reading the notes on a page and actually playing them. Similarly, leaders and their teams must dive into the data, wrestle with it, and discover its secrets firsthand. This could mean analyzing sales data to uncover buying trends or scrutinizing customer feedback for patterns. The key is to learn by doing.

But perhaps the most crucial element in cultivating an analytical mindset and data literacy is fostering a culture of curiosity and continuous learning. This doesn't happen overnight. It requires leaders to lead by example, to ask questions, to admit when they don't have the answers, and to always, always be learning. It's about creating an environment where questions are encouraged, where failure is seen not as a setback but as a stepping stone, and where every piece of data is a puzzle waiting to be solved.

Consider the story of a tech company that, on the brink of bankruptcy, turned its fortunes around by embracing data literacy. The CEO, once rigid in his decision-making, learned to question his assumptions. He encouraged his team to do the same, to challenge the status quo. They analyzed customer data like never before, uncovering insights that led to a revamped product line. The result? A dramatic turnaround in sales.

This story illustrates a powerful point. Data literacy and an analytical mindset are not just about crunching numbers. They're about transforming the way we think, leading with curiosity, and leveraging information for strategic advantage.

But beware, for data can be a double-edged sword. Without the critical thinking to interpret it correctly, it can lead to misguided conclusions. That's why leaders must not only be data literate themselves but also instill these values in their teams. It's a journey that requires persistence, curiosity, and a willingness to learn.

Let's not forget the significance of fostering a culture that values data literacy. It's akin to tending a garden. Just as the right soil, sunlight, and water are crucial for plants to thrive, so too is an environment that encourages questioning, learning, and growth essential for cultivating an analytical mindset.

In conclusion, as we navigate the age of data, let us remember that it is not just about having access to information but about harnessing it for strategic advantage. This requires an analytical mindset, statistical competence, and the ability to question and interpret data insights critically. Leaders who cultivate these skills in themselves and their teams will not only survive but thrive in this new era.

Visionary Thinking and Ability to Extract Strategic Insights

In the ever-evolving landscape of the digital age, a new breed of leaders has emerged. Visionary thinkers, these individuals possess the uncanny ability to sift through mountains of data to extract strategic insights that propel their organizations into the future. Their foresight disrupts industries and carves out new markets, setting the stage for a generation of innovation and transformation.

A visionary leader gazes upon the vast expanse of information not as an intimidating ocean of numbers but as a treasure trove of opportunities. They see patterns where others see chaos, potential where others see problems. But how do they accomplish this feat? What sets these leaders apart in their ability to harness information for strategic advantage?

Firstly, these leaders have a profound understanding of the business landscape. Like master chess players, they anticipate moves several steps ahead, considering not only the current state of play but also how the board might look several moves in the future. They study market trends, competitor behavior, and consumer preferences with a keen eye, always asking, "What's next?"

But understanding alone is not enough. Visionary leaders couple this knowledge with a creative mindset that dares to imagine the impossible. They ask audacious questions: "What if we could change the game entirely? What if there's a solution no one has thought of yet?" This creative spark is what fuels innovation, enabling them to envision future possibilities that others might dismiss as fanciful.

Consider the story of a leader who revolutionized the retail industry by envisioning a world where shopping could be done from the comfort of one's home, bypassing the need for physical stores. This leader, drawing upon data showing increasing internet usage and a growing demand for convenience, dared to dream of an online marketplace. Critics were skeptical, questioning the viability of such a model. Yet, by extracting strategic insights from data and coupling them with a bold vision, this leader disrupted the retail industry, creating a new market that forever changed how we shop.

How, then, can leaders cultivate the ability to extract and act on strategic insights from data? It begins with fostering a culture of curiosity and continuous learning within their organizations. Encourage your team to explore data, to question assumptions, and to look beyond the surface. Create an environment where innovative thinking is not just welcomed but celebrated.

Moreover, visionary leaders invest in developing their team's skills in data analysis and statistical reasoning. They understand that the ability to interpret data correctly is critical in making informed decisions. By empowering their teams with the tools and knowledge to analyze data effectively, they build a foundation for strategic insight extraction.

But visionary thinking is not just about having the right tools or skills. It requires a shift in mindset. Visionary leaders embrace uncertainty and are not afraid to take calculated risks. They understand that in the uncertainty lies the opportunity for breakthrough innovation.

So, ask yourself, do you view data as merely a tool for operational decisions, or do you see it as a compass guiding you toward future possibilities? Are you content with playing within the existing rules, or are you ready to redefine the game?

Visionary leaders are the architects of the future. They harness the power of data not just to navigate the present but to shape what lies ahead. Their ability to extract strategic insights from information propels their organizations to new heights, creating value and making an indelible mark on the world.

In this age of data, let us embrace the challenge to think differently, to dream boldly, and to lead with vision. The future awaits those daring enough to shape it.

In the words of a visionary leader, "The best way to predict the future is to invent it." Let this be our mantra as we navigate the uncharted waters of the digital age, harnessing information for strategic advantage.

Decisiveness Backed by Data-Driven Evidence

In an era where the sheer volume of information can be overwhelming, decisiveness emerges as a critical trait for effective leadership. Yet, the path to decisiveness is not paved with hasty conclusions or impulsive choices; it is informed by solid, data-driven evidence. The balance between swift decision-making and the rigorous analysis of data is a tightrope that leaders must learn to walk with precision. This chapter delves into the nuances of crafting a leadership style that is both decisive and deeply rooted in the analysis of data, highlighting strategies to manage the uncertainties that accompany predictive insights and emphasizing the importance of agility and adaptability.

Imagine standing at a crossroads, where each path represents a potential decision. The ground beneath is not stable; it shifts with the weight of new information and data that floods in with each passing moment. Leaders must make a choice – but not in haste. They must weigh their options, informed by the light of data that illuminates the paths ahead. This moment encapsulates the essence of leadership in the age of data.

Decisiveness, in this context, is not about the speed of making decisions but the quality and the confidence with which they are made. A leader's ability to sift through data, to identify what is relevant, and to apply it in decision-making processes is what sets them apart. But how does one achieve this balance? How does a leader become both decisive and data-driven?

The first step is developing a keen understanding of the data at one's disposal. This doesn't mean drowning in every piece of data available but rather identifying key indicators that are most relevant to the decision at hand. Prioritization is crucial. Not all data is created equal, and recognizing the data that truly matters can clear the fog that often surrounds complex decisions.

Once the relevant data is identified, the next challenge is interpretation. Data, in its raw form, can be misleading. Leaders must hone their ability to interpret data accurately, understanding its implications and the story it tells. This requires a deep engagement with the data, a willingness to question assumptions, and an openness to discover insights that may challenge preconceived notions.

But what about the uncertainties? Predictive insights, by nature, are not certainties. They are educated guesses about what the future holds, based on the patterns and trends observed in the data. Herein lies a significant challenge for leaders: making decisions when the future is not clear-cut. It requires a delicate balance – being bold enough to make decisions based on predictive insights but cautious enough to know that these decisions come with inherent risks.

Risk management becomes a critical skill in this environment. Leaders must not only be comfortable with taking calculated risks but also adept at preparing for potential outcomes. This involves scenario planning – envisioning different outcomes based on the decision made and developing strategies to address each possible scenario.

Agility and adaptability are the hallmarks of a leader who can navigate the uncertainties of data-driven decision-making. The landscape of information is ever-changing, and new data can emerge that challenges previous assumptions. Leaders must be prepared to pivot, to reassess their decisions in light of new information, and to steer their organizations in a new direction if necessary.

Consider the CEO who, informed by data, decides to pivot their company's strategy towards a new market. The decision, based on a thorough analysis of market trends and consumer behavior, is bold but calculated. Yet, as the strategy unfolds, new data emerges that suggests a shift in consumer preferences. An agile leader recognizes this shift, reassesses the decision, and adapts the strategy accordingly. This agility not only mitigates risk but also positions the company to capitalize on new opportunities.

In conclusion, leadership in the age of data is not just about having access to information; it's about how that information is used to make decisions. Decisiveness, informed by solid data-driven evidence, is a powerful tool in a leader's arsenal. It requires a deep engagement with data, an ability to manage uncertainties, and the agility to adapt in response to new information. Leaders who master this balance are not just navigating the present; they are shaping the future.

As we forge ahead, let us remember that decisiveness, backed by data-driven evidence, is not just a strategy. It's a mindset. It's the courage to make informed decisions, the wisdom to manage risks, and the flexibility to adapt when the world changes course. This is the essence of leadership in the age of data.

Inspiring and Leading Data-Driven Teams

In the labyrinth of the modern business world, where data is the Minotaur, leaders are the Theseus, required not only to navigate but to conquer. To triumph, they must not only wield the sword of decisiveness but also the shield of inspiration, especially when it comes to steering the ship of data-driven teams. This chapter explores the art and science of inspiring and leading teams in an era where data reigns supreme, focusing on strategies that foster a culture of data-driven excellence.

Leading by example stands as the cornerstone of inspiring a data-centric culture. Imagine a leader who not only preaches the gospel of data but lives by it. Every decision, no matter how small, is informed by data. This leader, much like a gardener, plants the seeds of curiosity and nurtures them with the water of knowledge and the sunlight of transparency. By doing so, they illuminate the path for their team, showing that data is not a distant deity to be feared but a tool to be wielded with precision and confidence.

Creating opportunities for skill development is another pillar in the temple of data-driven leadership. Consider the vast ocean of data that surrounds us; to navigate these waters, one must not only understand the currents but also know how to sail. Leaders must therefore equip their teams with the compass of data literacy, offering training and resources that empower team members to analyze, interpret, and leverage data. This empowerment transforms the team from passive passengers to active navigators, charting their course through the data deluge.

Encouragement of experimentation and learning from failures is the wind that propels the ship forward. In the realm of data, not every hypothesis will prove correct, and not every analysis will yield expected results. But within these failures lie golden opportunities for growth and learning. Leaders who celebrate these moments, who dissect failures with the precision of a surgeon but the compassion of a mentor, foster a culture of resilience. They teach their teams that every setback is a step forward, every mistake a milestone in the journey of discovery.

Recognizing and rewarding data-driven achievements is the treasure at the end of the quest. In a world often blinded by the glare of gut feelings and intuition, leaders must shine a spotlight on successes born from data. Whether it's a team member who uncovers a trend that leads to a breakthrough strategy or a group that leverages data to drive efficiencies, their achievements must be heralded. These moments of recognition serve as beacons, guiding and encouraging others to embark on their data-driven adventures.

But how does one weave these strategies into the fabric of their leadership style? The answer lies in the power of stories. Humans are narrative creatures, and stories are the threads that connect us. Leaders should strive to become storytellers, weaving tales of data-driven triumphs and lessons learned from failures. These stories, shared in team meetings or informal gatherings, become the lore of the organization, inspiring others to contribute their chapters.

Furthermore, leaders must foster an environment where questions are the currency of growth. Encourage team members to ask not just how things are done, but why. Why is this data important? Why does it matter to our project, our company, our customers? These questions ignite the spark of curiosity, driving individuals to dig deeper, to understand not just the 'what' but the 'why' and the 'how'.

In this age of data, the role of a leader transcends the traditional boundaries of management. Leaders become guides, mentors, and champions of a data-driven ethos. They recognize that in the vast sea of information, the compass of data literacy, the sails of experimentation, and the anchor of recognition are what will navigate their teams to success.

This journey is not without its challenges, but the rewards are manifold. Data-driven teams are not just efficient; they are innovative, resilient, and prepared to face the uncertainties of the future. Leaders who embrace this shift, who inspire and nurture their teams in the art of data, are not just leading for today. They are paving the way for a future where data is not just a tool but a compass, guiding decisions, strategies, and ultimately, success.

Let us embark on this journey with the knowledge that our efforts today will shape the leaders of tomorrow. In the age of data, the role of leadership is not just to lead but to inspire, to empower, and to illuminate the path forward. The future is data-driven, and together, we have the power to harness this force, turning information into strategic advantage.

The Data Landscape

Types of Data: Structured, Unstructured, and Semi-Structured

In the sprawling digital ecosystem, data emerges as the lifeblood, pulsating through the veins of modern enterprises. This chapter delves into the heart of data's anatomy, dissecting its types into structured, unstructured, and semi-structured categories. Understanding these distinctions is not merely academic; it's a strategic imperative for businesses aiming to harness information for a competitive edge.

Imagine, if you will, a vast library. In one section, books are meticulously organized by genre, author, and title - a testament to order. This is akin to structured data: highly organized and easily searchable, residing in relational databases and spreadsheets. It's the type of data that fits neatly into predefined models, like names in a phone book or product listings in an inventory.

Now, wander into a different part of the library, where manuscripts, letters, and diaries are strewn haphazardly. This is the realm of unstructured data: diverse, unorganized, and challenging to sift through. It includes everything from emails and social media posts to videos and images. For businesses, unstructured data is a treasure trove of insights into customer behavior and preferences, albeit one that's not easily unlocked.

LEADERSHIP IN THE AGE OF DATA: HARNESSING INFORMATION FOR STRATEGIC ADVANTAGE

Between these two extremes lies a hybrid zone, the domain of semi-structured data. Picture a room where some books are neatly shelved, while others lay in loose piles. Semi-structured data has some organizational properties but doesn't fit into a rigid structure. Examples include JSON and XML files, which, while not as orderly as a database, aren't as chaotic as a collection of tweets.

Why does this matter? The ability to classify data into these types is the first step in leveraging it for strategic decision-making. Structured data, with its ease of access and analysis, is often the first port of call for businesses seeking quick insights. Sales figures, inventory levels, and customer demographics can be easily mined for patterns and trends.

Unstructured data, however, holds the key to deeper, more nuanced insights. Through advanced analytical techniques, such as natural language processing and image recognition, businesses can uncover sentiments, preferences, and behaviors hidden within texts and visuals. The challenge lies in the complexity of analysis, demanding more sophisticated tools and skills.

Semi-structured data straddles these two worlds, offering a compromise between order and chaos. It's particularly relevant in the age of web data, where JSON and XML formats dominate. Here, businesses find a middle ground, tapping into structured attributes while accommodating more flexible data elements.

The implications for data analysis and decision-making are profound. Structured data, with its predictability, lends itself to traditional statistical analysis and reporting. It's the backbone of operational decision-making, supporting everything from financial forecasting to supply chain optimization.

Unstructured data, by contrast, demands a more exploratory approach. It's here that artificial intelligence and machine learning come into play, transforming raw text and images into actionable insights. The potential applications are boundless, from sentiment analysis in customer feedback to trend spotting in social media.

Semi-structured data, with its blend of characteristics, offers a versatile resource for businesses. It supports a range of analyses, from straightforward queries to complex data integrations. This flexibility makes it invaluable for tasks that require a mix of structured order and the rich context of unstructured data.

But here's the rub: managing and analyzing these diverse data types is no small feat. It requires a robust data strategy, cutting-edge technology, and, perhaps most critically, a skilled team of data professionals. The journey from data to decision is fraught with challenges, from ensuring data quality to protecting privacy.

Yet, the rewards are undeniable. In an era where information is both weapon and currency, mastering the art of data management and analysis is a strategic imperative. Businesses that can navigate the complexities of structured, unstructured, and semi-structured data stand to gain a formidable advantage in the competitive landscape.

Consider this: every piece of data, whether a neatly organized spreadsheet cell, a chaotic tweet, or a semi-structured JSON file, holds a piece of the puzzle. The art and science of data management lie in assembling these pieces into a coherent picture that informs strategic decisions.

In conclusion, the types of data - structured, unstructured, and semi-structured - form the building blocks of information management. Their effective analysis can illuminate paths to innovation, efficiency, and customer engagement. As businesses continue to grapple with the deluge of data, understanding these distinctions is not just beneficial; it's essential.

The question then becomes, how can your business turn this knowledge into action? The answer lies in embracing the diversity of data, investing in the right technologies and talent, and fostering a culture of data-driven decision-making. For in the age of data, knowledge is not just power; it's a strategic advantage waiting to be harnessed.

Sources of Data: Internal, External, and IoT Devices

In a world awash with information, discerning the sources of data that feed the ever-hungry analytics engines is a voyage of discovery. This chapter sails into the exploration of the vast seas of data sources, categorizing them into three broad archipelagos: internal databases, external datasets, and the burgeoning islands of IoT (Internet of Things) devices. These sources, when strategically integrated, offer businesses a panoramic view of the landscape, enhancing operations and uncovering new horizons of opportunity.

At the heart of every organization beats a pulse of data generated from within. Internal databases, the repositories of structured data, stand as the bedrock of this information. Picture a warehouse brimming with rows upon rows of neatly labeled crates, each containing valuable assets. Similarly, internal databases store a wealth of transactional records, customer information, employee details, and financial figures - each a potential gold mine of insights.

However, the challenge doesn't lie in the accumulation of this data but in its interpretation. How can one transform these raw numbers and facts into strategic intelligence? The key is in the integration of this data with other sources, weaving a tapestry that tells a more comprehensive story of the organization's operations and opportunities.

Gazing beyond the confines of an organization, external datasets stand as windows offering views of the vast world outside. These sources are as diverse as the ocean is deep, ranging from public government records and industry reports to social media trends and market research. They hold the keys to understanding the broader context in which a business operates – the competitive landscape, economic indicators, and consumer sentiments.

LEADERSHIP IN THE AGE OF DATA: HARNESSING INFORMATION FOR STRATEGIC ADVANTAGE

But how does one harness this plethora of information without drowning in it? The art lies in discerning relevance and authenticity. Not all external data is created equal, and its strategic integration requires a discerning eye for quality and applicability. When skillfully selected, this data complements internal sources, providing a richer, more nuanced perspective on strategic planning.

In the realm of IoT, objects come alive with data. From smart thermostats and fitness trackers to connected vehicles and industrial sensors, IoT devices are the sentinels at the edge of the network, gathering real-time data on a scale and scope previously unimaginable. They offer a pulse on the present, a continuous stream of insights into how products and services are being used, how they're performing, and how they're interacting with the environment around them.

Imagine a fleet of trucks equipped with GPS trackers and cargo sensors. Each vehicle becomes a node in a vast network, transmitting data on location, speed, fuel efficiency, and load status. This information, when analyzed, can revolutionize logistics and supply chain management, optimizing routes, reducing fuel consumption, and ensuring timely deliveries.

The true power of these diverse data sources lies not in their individual capabilities but in their strategic integration. Like a maestro conducting an orchestra, the savvy business leader must harmonize internal databases, external datasets, and IoT insights to create a symphony of strategic intelligence.

But what does this integration look like in practice? It begins with a clear vision of the objectives. What are the key questions the organization seeks to answer? From there, it's a matter of selecting the right instruments – the data sources that best address those questions – and tuning them to play in concert. Advanced analytics and machine learning algorithms serve as the conductor's baton, extracting patterns, trends, and predictions from the combined data.

The strategic integration of diverse data sources opens doors to improved decision-making, innovative business models, and competitive advantage. It enables organizations to operate with greater agility, adapting to changes in the market, consumer behavior, and technology with unprecedented speed and precision.

Yet, this journey is not without its challenges. It requires a robust infrastructure, sophisticated analytics capabilities, and, above all, a culture that values and understands the power of data. The questions that arise are manifold: How can we ensure the privacy and security of this data? How do we navigate the ethical implications of its use? And how do we foster the skills and mindset needed to leverage it effectively?

As we stand on the brink of this new era of data-driven leadership, these are the questions that will shape the future. The organizations that can navigate this complex landscape, harnessing the strategic potential of internal, external, and IoT data sources, will be the ones to lead the way into the age of data. The horizon is vast, and the opportunities limitless.

The call to action is clear: Embrace the diversity of data. Invest in the technologies and talent needed to harness it. And embark on the journey of strategic integration with curiosity, courage, and a vision for the future.

In the age of data, the path to leadership is paved with information. The question is, are you ready to take the first step?

Big Data Technologies: An Overview of Tools and Platforms

In an era where the digital footprint of organizations expands by the second, understanding the landscape of big data technologies becomes not just beneficial but imperative. These tools and platforms are the pillars supporting the vast edifice of data-driven decision-making. They collect, store, process, and analyze the deluge of data that modern businesses generate and encounter. For leaders aiming to steer their organizations towards strategic advantage, the mastery of these technologies is a crucial skill.

Before diving into the ocean of analytics, one must first understand how to gather and house the waves of data. Data collection and storage technologies form the bedrock of the big data landscape. Imagine a vast library, its shelves stretching into the horizon, each book brimming with stories waiting to be told. Similarly, technologies like Hadoop Distributed File System (HDFS) and Amazon S3 offer scalable, secure platforms for storing massive datasets – the raw narratives of the digital world.

Yet, the challenge lies not merely in storage but in doing so efficiently and accessibly. Solutions such as NoSQL databases, including MongoDB and Cassandra, break away from traditional relational database models to offer more flexible schemas suitable for the unstructured nature of big data. They allow for the rapid retrieval and manipulation of data, ensuring that the information is not just stored but ready to be harnessed.

With the data securely housed, the next step is processing – the crucible where raw data is transformed into actionable insights. Here, technologies like Apache Spark and Apache Flink come to the forefront. They process large datasets at lightning speeds, performing complex analytics that turn the raw data into refined, valuable information.

Consider a miner sifting through soil and rock to find precious metals. In a similar vein, these processing technologies sift through the raw, unstructured data, identifying patterns, trends, and anomalies. They enable businesses to distill vast datasets into meaningful insights, powering everything from operational improvements to strategic initiatives.

Analysis technologies bring clarity and focus, allowing leaders to view their organizations through the lens of data-driven insights. Tools such as Python, with its rich ecosystem of libraries like Pandas and NumPy, offer powerful capabilities for data analysis and manipulation. Meanwhile, specialized platforms like Tableau and Power BI provide interactive visualizations, transforming complex datasets into intuitive, accessible insights.

LEADERSHIP IN THE AGE OF DATA: HARNESSING INFORMATION FOR STRATEGIC ADVANTAGE

Imagine standing atop a mountain, surveying the landscape below through a powerful telescope. Just as the telescope brings distant features into sharp relief, these analysis tools highlight opportunities and challenges within the data, guiding strategic decision-making.

As the big data landscape evolves, two trends stand out for their transformative potential: cloud computing and AI-driven analytics platforms.

Cloud computing, with services like AWS, Microsoft Azure, and Google Cloud, offers scalable, flexible resources for handling big data. It removes the constraints of physical infrastructure, allowing organizations to adjust their computing power and storage capacity with the ebb and flow of their data needs. This elasticity, combined with the pay-as-you-go pricing model, makes cloud computing an attractive proposition for businesses of all sizes.

On the horizon, AI-driven analytics platforms promise to revolutionize how organizations derive insights from their data. These platforms, leveraging machine learning and artificial intelligence, automate the discovery of patterns and predictions, offering insights that might elude even the most skilled analysts. They represent not just a tool but a collaborator in the quest for strategic advantage, a co-pilot navigating the complex skies of the data landscape.

With such an array of tools and platforms, how do leaders choose the right ones for their organizations? The answer lies in a clear-eyed assessment of needs, capabilities, and strategic objectives. It requires leaders to ask probing questions: What are our most pressing data challenges? How can we scale our data infrastructure to meet future needs? What balance must we strike between flexibility and security?

Selecting the right big data technologies is a strategic decision, one that shapes the organization's ability to harness information for competitive advantage. It demands a thorough understanding of the available tools and a vision for how they can be integrated into the broader strategy of the organization.

The journey through the landscape of big data technologies is both daunting and exhilarating. It offers the promise of strategic insights and operational efficiencies, the potential to not just navigate but shape the future of industries. The tools and platforms discussed herein are the compasses and maps guiding that journey.

For leaders in the age of data, the call to action is clear: Embrace the technologies that gather, store, process, and analyze the vast seas of data. Navigate the evolving trends with an eye towards scalability, security, and innovation. And, most importantly, wield these tools with strategic acumen, harnessing information for competitive advantage.

The age of data beckons. The tools are at your disposal. The question that remains is, how will you lead your organization into this new era?

Data Governance and Ethics

Navigating Ethical Considerations of Data Usage

In the digital era, where data flows like the lifeblood of our society, navigating the ethical considerations of data usage emerges as a paramount challenge for leaders. The vast oceans of information, once harnessed, hold the power to transform industries, economies, and lives. Yet, with great power comes great responsibility. Ethical dilemmas loom large over the horizon, casting shadows on the potential benefits of data analytics.

Imagine, for a moment, the allure of data analytics. Picture a world where predictive algorithms can pinpoint the next market trend, personalize education to the learning pace of each student, or even save lives through early disease detection. The possibilities stretch to the horizon, a testament to human ingenuity.

However, beneath this glittering surface lies a darker underbelly. Privacy concerns whisper warnings as personal information becomes the currency of the digital age. Data breaches scream headlines, shaking the trust of consumers. The responsible use of data analytics becomes not just a strategic advantage but a moral imperative.

Leaders, standing at the helm of this new frontier, face a complex web of ethical considerations. How do they navigate this terrain, where the line between innovation and intrusion blurs?

Privacy concerns demand our immediate attention. In an age where personal details are keystrokes away from public exposure, respecting individual privacy rights is non-negotiable. Leaders must ask themselves, "Are we protecting our users' data as if it were our own?" This question serves as a guiding star, steering the ship away from the jagged rocks of exploitation and towards the safe harbor of trust and respect.

Data security, equally critical, forms the backbone of ethical data usage. A single breach can erode years of trust, a cost no organization can afford. Robust security measures become the shields protecting the kingdom of data. Leaders must fortify these defenses, vigilant against the ever-evolving threats that prowl the digital landscape.

The responsible use of data analytics, however, extends beyond privacy and security. It encompasses the integrity of the data itself and the decisions derived from it. Misleading data or biased algorithms can lead to decisions that disproportionately harm certain groups or individuals. Leaders bear the responsibility of ensuring the data's integrity, questioning not just the accuracy but the fairness of their analytic tools.

Establishing ethical guidelines and practices, therefore, becomes the beacon for navigating these murky waters. These guidelines, rooted in respect for individual rights and a commitment to security, must be more than mere words on a page. They should embody the organization's values, informing every decision, every project, every innovation.

Transparency plays a crucial role in this ethical framework. Openly sharing how data is collected, used, and protected fosters trust among stakeholders. It invites dialogue, encouraging questions and concerns to surface. This openness, in turn, strengthens the bond between organizations and their users, building a foundation of mutual respect and understanding.

Leaders must also cultivate a culture of responsibility within their organizations. This culture empowers every employee to act as a guardian of data ethics, vigilant against practices that compromise ethical standards. Training programs, regular assessments, and open forums can nurture this culture, embedding ethical considerations into the fabric of the organization.

In the quest for strategic advantage, the ethical use of data stands as a pillar of sustainable success. It's a testament to the organization's integrity, a magnet for trust, and a catalyst for innovation.

Reflect for a moment on the profound impact of ethical leadership in the age of data. Imagine a future where data not only drives growth but does so with a deep respect for the dignity of every individual. This future is not just possible; it is essential.

Leaders, the compass is in your hands. The course you set today will shape the world of tomorrow. Will you navigate these ethical considerations with wisdom and foresight, harnessing information for strategic advantage while honoring the rights and trust of those you serve?

The journey is complex, fraught with challenges, but the destination—a world where data enriches lives without compromising ethics—is worth every effort.

This is your moment. Lead the way.

Understanding Data Privacy Laws and Regulations

In the labyrinth of the digital age, data privacy laws and regulations stand as the guardians of integrity, fairness, and respect. These legal frameworks are not merely hurdles to overcome; they are the very foundation upon which trust between organizations and individuals is built. But what are these laws, and how do they shape the way leaders must navigate the ocean of information at their disposal?

Globally, the General Data Protection Regulation (GDPR) serves as a beacon, illuminating the path toward stringent data protection. Enacted by the European Union in 2018, GDPR has set a global benchmark for data privacy, impacting not only European companies but any organization dealing with EU citizens' data. Its core principles revolve around consent, transparency, and the individual's right to access, correct, and erase their personal data. Picture a world where every piece of personal information is treated with the utmost respect, where consent must be freely given, specific, informed, and unambiguous. This is the world GDPR aims to create.

Across the Atlantic, the United States presents a patchwork of state-specific regulations, with California's Consumer Privacy Act (CCPA) leading the charge. As a pioneering state-level law, the CCPA empowers consumers with the right to know about the personal data collected by businesses, the purpose of collection, and with whom it is shared. Envision a marketplace where transparency reigns supreme, where consumers hold the keys to their digital footprint.

In the vast lands of Asia, the Personal Data Protection Act (PDPA) in Singapore offers a comprehensive approach to data privacy, balancing the need for data protection with the need for economic growth. It mandates organizations to appoint a data protection officer, ensuring a dedicated guardian of privacy within the corporate structure. Imagine a business landscape where privacy is not just a legal requirement but a strategic role within every company.

Turning our gaze to Brazil, the Lei Geral de Proteção de Dados (LGPD) echoes the comprehensive nature of GDPR, underscoring the global trend towards more stringent data privacy measures. Through its emphasis on data subject rights and the accountability of data processors and controllers, LGPD paints a future where personal data is handled with care, regardless of borders.

But why does compliance matter? The consequences of non-compliance are not merely financial; they strike at the very heart of trust. Consider the fallout from a data breach or misuse of personal information. It's not just the immediate financial penalty but the long-lasting damage to an organization's reputation. Leaders, therefore, play a crucial role in ensuring adherence to these laws, embodying the principles of integrity and respect that form the bedrock of data privacy.

Compliance begins with understanding. Leaders must invest time and resources into comprehensively understanding the legal landscape, tailoring their data protection strategies to meet these varied requirements. A one-size-fits-all approach falls short in a world where data privacy laws differ by jurisdiction.

But compliance is more than just a checkbox. It's a commitment to ethical leadership. Imagine a culture where every employee, from the boardroom to the front lines, views data protection as paramount. This culture is fostered by leaders who prioritize training, who lead by example, and who embed data privacy into the DNA of their organization.

The role of leadership extends beyond mere compliance; it's about pioneering a future where data privacy is viewed not as a constraint but as a strategic advantage. In a world weary of breaches and misuse, trust becomes a currency more valuable than data itself. Leaders who champion data privacy laws and regulations not only navigate the legal landscape but also chart a course towards lasting relationships with customers, built on the solid ground of trust and respect.

So, where does your organization stand? Are you merely reacting to the ever-changing world of data privacy laws, or are you proactively shaping a culture that elevates privacy as a cornerstone of your strategic advantage?

This is not just a question of legal compliance. It's a question of leadership. In the age of data, leading with integrity, respect, and a deep commitment to privacy is the hallmark of true strategic advantage. Leaders, the choice is yours. Will you rise to the challenge?

Implementing Practices for Ethical Data Management

In the digital era, where data flows as freely as water, the need for ethical data management practices has never been more critical. As leaders, the responsibility to harness this flow, ensuring it nourishes rather than drowns, falls squarely on our shoulders. It's a daunting task, yet, with the right approach, it can be the source of unparalleled strategic advantage.

Imagine a building, towering and intricate. Without a solid foundation, it's vulnerable to the merest gust of wind. Similarly, an organization's data practices require a robust framework to stand firm against the ever-present threats of misuse and breach. Crafting such a framework begins with understanding the very data we seek to protect.

What kind of data does your organization handle? Is it sensitive, personal, or perhaps a mix? Recognizing the nature of your data is the first step toward effective governance.

Following this, the establishment of clear policies on data acquisition, storage, usage, and deletion is paramount. These policies, however, aren't static; they're living documents that adapt as new challenges and opportunities arise.

Within the heart of ethical data management beats a key player: the Data Protection Officer (DPO). This role, mandated by laws such as the GDPR, acts as the guardian and advocate for data privacy within an organization. But what does a DPO do, exactly?

Primarily, the DPO oversees compliance with data protection laws, serving as the bridge between regulatory bodies, the organization, and the public. They conduct regular audits, train staff, and provide crucial advice on data protection impact assessments. In essence, the DPO embodies the organization's commitment to data privacy, ensuring that ethical considerations are never sidelined in the quest for innovation.

At the core of ethical data management lies a culture that values accountability and transparency. But how can such a culture be fostered? It starts at the top. Leaders must embody the principles they wish to see, demonstrating a genuine commitment to ethical practices in every decision and policy.

Engaging employees in regular training sessions not only educates but also empowers them to take personal responsibility for data protection. Moreover, transparency with customers and stakeholders builds trust, showing that

LEADERSHIP IN THE AGE OF DATA: HARNESSING INFORMATION FOR STRATEGIC ADVANTAGE

their data is not only respected but valued. Remember, trust is the foundation upon which long-term relationships are built.

1. Begin with a thorough assessment of the data you hold. Map its flow through your organization to identify potential risks and areas for improvement.

2. Based on your assessment, develop comprehensive data management policies. These should cover every aspect of the data lifecycle, from collection to deletion.

3. If your organization is large enough or handles sensitive data, appointing a DPO is not just a legal requirement but a strategic move. Ensure they have the authority and resources to effect change.

4. Implement ongoing training programs for all employees. Make data protection part of the onboarding process for new hires.

5. Regularly communicate with your stakeholders about how their data is being used. Be open about your practices and how you protect their information.

6. Conduct regular audits of your data management practices. This will help you stay compliant and identify areas for improvement.

7. Have a clear, actionable plan in place for data breaches. Quick and transparent response can mitigate damage and maintain trust.

Embarking on the journey of ethical data management is no small feat. It requires commitment, resources, and a shift in organizational culture. Yet, the rewards far outweigh the challenges. In an age where data breaches can erode trust overnight, being a beacon of integrity and respect can set you apart.

Let's not forget, data doesn't just represent numbers or entries in a database; it represents people. Their preferences, behaviors, and personal information. Treating this data with the care it deserves is not just a legal obligation but a moral one.

As leaders, we hold the power to shape the future of data management. A future where data is not just a tool for strategic advantage but a symbol of our commitment to ethical practices and respect for privacy.

In the end, the question isn't whether we can afford to implement these practices. The real question is, can we afford not to?

Ethical data management is the cornerstone of trust in the digital age. It's time we rise to the challenge.

Building Trust and Transparency in Data Practices

In an era dominated by data, the pillars of trust and transparency in data practices have emerged as indispensable elements for organizational success. These principles act as the bedrock upon which companies can build a formidable reputation, fostering an environment where strategic advantage

LEADERSHIP IN THE AGE OF DATA: HARNESSING INFORMATION FOR STRATEGIC ADVANTAGE

is not just a goal but a reality. This chapter delves deep into the essence of building trust and transparency, unraveling the layers that constitute effective data communication and the pivotal role they play in enhancing stakeholder confidence.

Transparency in data practices should not be an afterthought; it must be woven into the very fabric of an organization's data management strategy. This begins with an open dialogue about the use of data. Imagine a company that not only collects data but also takes the time to explain how each dataset serves a purpose. Such clarity demystifies data operations for stakeholders, painting a clear picture of intent and application.

Notably, the journey toward transparency is punctuated with challenges. It demands a shift in mindset, from guarding data as a tightly kept secret to viewing it as a shared asset that benefits all. Yet, the rewards are manifold. Transparent practices lead to a harmonious relationship between organizations and their stakeholders, characterized by mutual respect and understanding.

Trust is the currency of the digital age. It's earned through consistent, ethical data practices that prioritize the privacy and security of stakeholder information. But how can organizations ensure they are deserving of this trust? The answer lies in the deliberate actions taken to safeguard data against breaches and misuse.

Consider the impact of implementing robust security measures and privacy policies that are not just compliant with regulations but exceed them. These actions send a powerful message about a company's dedication to protecting stakeholder interests. Moreover, when data is used responsibly to enhance services and tailor experiences, it reinforces the value exchange between a company and its users.

Clear communication about the benefits of data initiatives plays a crucial role in building stakeholder trust. When individuals understand how their data contributes to improvements in products, services, or user experience, it transforms their perception of data sharing from a potential risk to a valued contribution.

For example, a healthcare provider using patient data to improve treatment plans can significantly enhance patient outcomes. When communicated effectively, patients are more likely to support and participate in such data initiatives, recognizing the direct impact on their well-being.

Protecting data privacy is a formidable challenge in the quest for transparency. It requires a delicate balance between sharing information about data practices and ensuring sensitive details remain secure. Organizations must navigate this landscape with care, adopting a principle of 'privacy by design'—where privacy considerations are integrated into the development of business processes and systems from the ground up.

The implementation of end-to-end encryption, anonymization techniques, and stringent access controls are examples of proactive measures that reinforce a commitment to privacy. Furthermore, regular training for employees on data protection enhances an organization's ability to prevent breaches and respond effectively should one occur.

The implications of trust and transparency extend far beyond the immediate relationship between a company and its stakeholders. They contribute to a larger ecosystem of trust in technology and its role in society. In a landscape frequently marred by scandals and breaches, organizations that stand as beacons of integrity distinguish themselves.

Imagine a world where every company treated data with the respect it deserves. Such an environment would not only elevate the standard of data practices but also foster innovation and progress, powered by a shared commitment to ethical principles.

The path to building trust and transparency in data practices is both challenging and rewarding. It demands a steadfast commitment to ethical principles, a proactive approach to communication, and an unwavering focus on stakeholder well-being. Yet, the benefits—ranging from enhanced reputation to strategic advantage—are undeniable.

As we navigate the complexities of the digital age, let us remember the profound impact of our data practices. In the grand tapestry of data-driven innovation, trust and transparency are not just threads; they are the colors that give it life and meaning.

Let this be a call to action for leaders and organizations worldwide: to embrace the principles of trust and transparency, not as mere compliance obligations, but as core values that define the future of data management. Together, we can usher in an era where data serves as a bridge to understanding, cooperation, and shared success.

Integrating Data Analytics Into Decision Processes

Frameworks for Data-Informed Decision-Making

In an era where information is as abundant as it is dynamic, the art of making well-informed decisions has never been more critical. Enter the realm of data-informed decision-making, a practice that has transformed from a mere advantage into a necessity for leaders seeking strategic success. But how does one navigate this vast ocean of data to not merely float but sail swiftly towards their desired horizon? The answer lies in understanding and applying the right frameworks and methodologies.

At the heart of this journey is a series of steps designed to convert raw data into actionable insights. This process begins with data collection, a phase that requires precision and a keen eye for what is truly relevant amidst the noise. Picture a seasoned fisherman casting his net into the sea, not indiscriminately, but with an expert knowledge of where the finest fish swarm.

Following collection, data analysis takes center stage. This step is akin to the fisherman sorting his catch, separating the valuable from the mundane. Tools and techniques vary widely, from statistical analysis to machine learning algorithms, each offering a different lens through which to view the gathered information.

The third step, interpretation, demands a shift from the quantitative to the qualitative. Here, the fisherman must understand not just which fish he has caught, but what his catch says about the sea's changing conditions. Similarly, leaders must discern patterns and narratives within their data, crafting a story that speaks to the underlying truths of their operational environment.

Finally, application to decision-making processes represents the culmination of this journey. It is the moment when the fisherman, having understood the sea's messages, adjusts his strategies to ensure a bountiful catch. For leaders, it means integrating insights into strategic planning, ensuring decisions are not just reactions to the present but informed predictions of the future.

Within this overarching framework, several methodologies stand out for their effectiveness and adaptability. The Balanced Scorecard, for instance, enables organizations to view their operations through four critical lenses: financial performance, customer knowledge, internal business processes, and learning and growth. Imagine an architect considering not just the blueprint but the landscape, materials, and purpose of a building.

Another powerful tool is the SWOT Analysis, which invites leaders to examine their Strengths, Weaknesses, Opportunities, and Threats. It's akin to a general surveying the battlefield, understanding not just his army's capabilities but the terrain and the enemy's positioning.

LEADERSHIP IN THE AGE OF DATA: HARNESSING INFORMATION FOR STRATEGIC ADVANTAGE

Moreover, the Five Whys technique encourages a deeper exploration of issues, much like a curious child relentlessly questioning the world to understand its workings. By asking "why" repeatedly, one can peel away the layers of a problem, revealing its root cause.

But what about the vast seas of data that remain uncharted? Here, Big Data Analytics offers a compass. It allows for the analysis of extremely large datasets to uncover hidden patterns, correlations, and other insights. Imagine astronomers gazing into the cosmos, discovering not just stars but galaxies, each telling its own story of the universe.

Each of these frameworks and methodologies offers a pathway through the complex landscape of data-informed decision-making. Yet, they require not just knowledge, but wisdom in application. Remember, data alone does not hold the answer; it is the lens through which we view it that reveals the path to strategic advantage.

Consider this: when faced with a decision, how often do you rely solely on gut feeling or past experiences? While intuition and history are valuable guides, they are but a single thread in the tapestry of decision-making. Data offers a multitude of threads, each a different color and texture, waiting to be woven into a richer, more insightful picture.

Let's not forget, however, the human element. Data, for all its objectivity, cannot capture the nuance of human emotion, the unpredictability of behavior, or the complexity of societal trends. It serves not as a replacement for human judgment but as a complement, enhancing our understanding and guiding our choices.

In conclusion, the frameworks and methodologies for data-informed decision-making are as varied as they are vital. They serve as navigational aids in an ever-expanding sea of information, enabling leaders to chart a course towards strategic success. But remember, the map is not the territory. It is through the skillful integration of data insights with human intuition and experience that true strategic advantage is achieved.

As we navigate this age of data, let us do so with both caution and courage, aware of the power at our fingertips but mindful of the responsibility it entails. For in the end, it is not just about making decisions but making the right decisions for our organizations, our communities, and our future.

Overcoming Biases and Challenges in Data Interpretation

In the labyrinth of data interpretation, leaders often encounter invisible adversaries that skew their judgment and cloud their strategic vision. These foes, known as biases and challenges in data interpretation, can lead decision-makers astray, compelling them to see mirages in deserts of information. To navigate through this treacherous terrain, it becomes imperative to recognize these biases and arm oneself with strategies to mitigate their effects.

LEADERSHIP IN THE AGE OF DATA: HARNESSING INFORMATION FOR STRATEGIC ADVANTAGE

Imagine a sculptor, chiseling away at a block of marble. Each strike is guided by the vision of the masterpiece that lies within, yet the sculptor must constantly battle the flaws and fissures in the stone that threaten to mar the final creation. Similarly, leaders must sculpt decisions from the raw marble of data, all the while contending with biases that lurk within.

Among the most insidious of these biases is the confirmation bias. This is the tendency to search for, interpret, and recall information in a way that confirms one's preconceptions, effectively wearing blinders that block out conflicting evidence. Like a detective convinced of a suspect's guilt, a leader may only seek data that supports their initial hypothesis, ignoring the broader picture.

Another formidable challenge is overfitting, a phenomenon akin to tailoring a suit to fit a mannequin so precisely that it cannot fit a real human being. In the context of data, overfitting occurs when a model or analysis is so closely aligned with a particular set of data, including its anomalies and noise, that it fails to predict future observations accurately. It's as if one tried to navigate a vast ocean using a map drawn from the waters of a single bay.

How, then, can leaders overcome these biases and challenges? The first step lies in assembling a team as diverse as the spectrum of colors in a sunset. A team that brings together varied perspectives, backgrounds, and areas of expertise can challenge entrenched viewpoints, shining a light on blind spots that a homogenous group might miss. Just as a choir blends different voices to create a harmony richer than any single note, a diverse team can synthesize multiple viewpoints into a more accurate interpretation of data.

Cross-validation of data insights emerges as another potent strategy. By testing and validating findings across different data sets or subsets, leaders can avoid the trap of overfitting. Think of it as a chef tasting a dish at different stages of its preparation; by sampling and adjusting, the chef ensures the final dish is delightful to a wide range of palates.

Fostering a culture of critical thinking and open dialogue acts as the keystone in the archway to overcoming biases. Encouraging team members to question assumptions, debate interpretations, and consider alternative viewpoints cultivates an environment where data is scrutinized from all angles. It's akin to turning a gemstone in the light, observing how it sparkles differently with each rotation.

Can you recall a time when a decision, seemingly well-founded on data, led you astray?

Chances are, biases played a role in that misstep. It's not just about having data but understanding its language, acknowledging its limitations, and listening to the quiet whispers of what it might not be saying.

Strategies abound for those willing to embark on this journey. From leveraging software tools designed to detect bias in data sets to implementing double-blind procedures in data analysis, the toolkit for combating bias is both varied and effective. Yet, the most powerful tool remains the human mind, capable of introspection, adaptation, and growth.

LEADERSHIP IN THE AGE OF DATA: HARNESSING INFORMATION FOR STRATEGIC ADVANTAGE

Incorporating these strategies into the decision-making process is not merely a recommendation; it is a call to arms in the age of data. For in this era, data is not just a resource—it is the very terrain upon which battles for strategic advantage are fought. Leaders who master the art of navigating this terrain, biases and all, will not only survive but thrive.

One must remember, data is like water—essential, powerful, but without form. It is the vessel of interpretation that gives it shape. Choose the right vessel, free from the distortions of bias, and the waters of data can carry you to new horizons of strategic success.

In conclusion, the journey through the age of data is fraught with challenges but ripe with opportunities. By recognizing and overcoming biases, leaders can harness information not as a crude tool, but as a precision instrument for carving out strategic advantage in a competitive landscape. Let this be your guide, a beacon in the dense fog of data, illuminating the path to informed, unbiased decision-making.

Case Studies: Success Stories of Data-Driven Leadership

Navigating through the vast ocean of information, leaders worldwide have embarked on journeys utilizing data as their compass. These pioneers in data-driven leadership have not only reached new heights of success but also set benchmarks for others to follow. Let's delve into the tales of these trailblazers, unraveling the strategies that guided them through the tempests of data to the calm shores of strategic advantage.

The Retail Giant's Revival: A Tale of Data-Driven Transformation

Once teetering on the brink of irrelevance, a renowned retail giant staged an extraordinary comeback, all thanks to a visionary leader who believed in the power of data analytics. Faced with dwindling sales and fierce competition, the company found its savior in a new CEO with a track record of leveraging data for strategic decisions.

The challenge was daunting. Traditional sales strategies and customer outreach programs were failing. The CEO's first order of business? Implementing a comprehensive data analytics program that could dissect every aspect of the business, from supply chain logistics to customer preferences.

Employing advanced analytics and machine learning algorithms, the team began to uncover insights that had previously been hidden. Inventory management was optimized, reducing waste and ensuring that popular products were always in stock. Personalized marketing campaigns, informed by data on customer behavior, led to an uptick in customer engagement and loyalty.

The outcome was nothing short of miraculous. Within a few years, the company not only reclaimed its position as a market leader but also saw its profits soar to new heights. The CEO's data-driven approach had transformed a struggling retailer into a powerhouse of innovation and efficiency.

The Healthcare Revolution: Saving Lives with Data

LEADERSHIP IN THE AGE OF DATA: HARNESSING INFORMATION FOR STRATEGIC ADVANTAGE

In the world of healthcare, decisions can mean the difference between life and death. One healthcare organization, led by a forward-thinking executive, embarked on a mission to revolutionize patient care through data analytics.

The executive faced a healthcare system riddled with inefficiencies and outdated practices. The strategy? To implement a data-driven approach to patient care, focusing on predictive analytics to prevent diseases and manage chronic conditions more effectively.

By integrating data from various sources, including electronic health records, wearable devices, and genomics, the organization developed models that could predict health risks with astonishing accuracy. These models enabled doctors to tailor treatments to the individual, improving outcomes and reducing the cost of care.

The results were groundbreaking. Hospital readmission rates plummeted, patient satisfaction scores reached all-time highs, and the organization became a beacon of innovation in healthcare.

The Manufacturing Marvel: Streamlining Operations with Data

In the competitive world of manufacturing, one company stood out for its commitment to data-driven excellence. The CEO, a firm believer in the power of data to drive efficiency, spearheaded the adoption of Internet of Things (IoT) technologies throughout the manufacturing process.

The challenge was immense. The manufacturing landscape was fraught with inefficiencies, from equipment downtime to supply chain disruptions. The CEO's solution? A network of sensors and smart devices that could monitor every aspect of the manufacturing process in real-time.

This IoT ecosystem collected vast amounts of data, which was then analyzed to identify bottlenecks and predict equipment failures before they happened. The company could now preemptively address issues, dramatically reducing downtime and improving production efficiency.

The transformation was profound. The company not only reduced its operational costs but also significantly improved its product quality, setting a new standard in manufacturing excellence.

Reflections: What Can We Learn?

These stories illuminate the path for leaders embarking on their own data-driven journeys. They underscore the importance of embracing data analytics, not as a mere tool, but as a strategic asset that can redefine an organization's future.

Yet, the road to data-driven leadership is not without its challenges. It requires a vision that transcends traditional boundaries, a willingness to invest in new technologies, and a culture that values data-driven decision-making.

As we reflect on these success stories, the question arises: How can we apply these lessons to our own organizations? How can

LEADERSHIP IN THE AGE OF DATA: HARNESSING INFORMATION FOR STRATEGIC ADVANTAGE

we harness the power of data to navigate the complexities of the modern business landscape?

The answers lie in the stories of those who dared to lead with data. For in the age of information, data is the beacon that guides us to strategic advantage.

Driving Innovation With Data

Fostering Innovation Through Data Insights

In a world inundated with data, the key to unlocking the doors of innovation lies not in the accumulation but in the astute interpretation of this digital wealth. As we navigate through the age of information, the art of discerning valuable insights from the vast expanse of data has become a pivotal skill for leaders aiming to steer their organizations toward uncharted territories of innovation.

Imagine a vast ocean, its depths teeming with undiscovered species, its currents hiding ancient wrecks filled with untold treasures. This ocean is the data that today's businesses have at their disposal. The challenge, however, is not in the gathering of this data - for the ocean is always there, vast and waiting - but in the diving deep, in the discovering of patterns, trends, and insights that lie hidden beneath the surface.

How, then, do organizations dive into this ocean and emerge with pearls of innovation?

The answer begins with predictive analytics. Like the seasoned captain of a ship who reads the stars to navigate the seas, predictive analytics enables businesses to forecast future trends based on historical data. But it's not just about predicting the future; it's about shaping it. By understanding what is likely to happen, companies can innovate proactively, designing products, services, and strategies that meet the future head-on.

Consider, for a moment, the story of a small online bookstore that transformed into the world's largest internet retailer. This metamorphosis was fueled by the company's ability to predict and adapt to consumer behavior, leveraging data insights to recommend products, streamline the shopping experience, and ultimately, innovate on logistics and delivery. The bookstore did not just sell books; it redefined retail.

But predictive analytics is just the beginning.

Customer segmentation takes this a step further, slicing the ocean of data into manageable streams, each representing a different segment of the market. By analyzing these segments, businesses can tailor their offerings to meet the specific needs and preferences of each group, creating a more personalized and engaging customer experience. This is not just innovation; this is innovation with precision.

Imagine a coffee shop that, through data insights, realizes its morning customers prefer quick, to-go orders, while afternoon patrons linger for the ambiance. By segmenting its customers and adapting its service and environment accordingly, the coffee shop innovates its business model, enhancing customer satisfaction and loyalty.

But fostering innovation through data insights is not without its challenges.

The sheer volume of data can be overwhelming, the tools complex, and the skills required specialized. Here, the importance of simplicity cannot be overstated. In the pursuit of innovation, clarity in data interpretation and actionability of insights are paramount. Complex data analyses must be distilled into understandable, actionable steps that can drive decision-making and innovation.

Moreover, innovation is not just about the new but also about the now.

How can businesses ensure that their innovations are not just novel but relevant and timely? The answer lies in the continuous monitoring of data, adapting to trends in real-time, and always being ready to pivot. Flexibility and agility become as important as the insights themselves.

Innovation, after all, is not a destination but a journey.

It requires curiosity, the willingness to explore the unknown, and the courage to fail and learn. Data insights serve as the compass on this journey, guiding decisions, inspiring new ideas, and illuminating the path to innovation.

But let's pause for a moment.

Have you ever considered the impact of a single insight? A pattern in consumer behavior, a gap in the market, a new way of using an existing product - these are the sparks that ignite the fires of innovation. And behind every spark is the careful analysis of data, the diligent search for something not yet seen, the relentless pursuit of knowledge.

LEADERSHIP IN THE AGE OF DATA: HARNESSING INFORMATION FOR STRATEGIC ADVANTAGE

Data insights do not just foster innovation; they fuel it.

In a world that is constantly changing, where tomorrow's needs are unknown, and today's solutions may be tomorrow's challenges, the ability to harness data for strategic advantage is invaluable. It is not just about having information but about knowing what to do with it, seeing what others do not, and daring to venture where others have not.

So, as we sail the vast ocean of data, let us not be daunted by its depth or overwhelmed by its expanse. Instead, let us dive deep, with eyes open for patterns, trends, and insights that can lead to innovation. For in this age of information, the true leaders are those who can turn data into strategic advantage, navigating their organizations toward new horizons of innovation and success.

In conclusion, the fostered innovation through data insights stands not merely as an option but as an imperative in the quest for competitive advantage and strategic success. As we continue to delve into the realms of predictive analytics, customer segmentation, and beyond, the potential for groundbreaking innovation stretches before us, limitless as the ocean itself.

Are you ready to dive in?

Exploring the Intersection of Data Analytics and Digital Transformation

Digital transformation, a phrase that echoes through the corridors of modern business, signifies more than just a shift towards a digital era; it represents a profound metamorphosis in how companies operate, innovate, and deliver value. At the heart of this transformation lies data analytics, a beacon guiding organizations through the murky waters of change. But how exactly does data analytics catalyze digital transformation, and what challenges and opportunities arise at this intersection?

In the journey of digital transformation, data analytics serves as the compass, enabling organizations to navigate through the complexities of modern markets with agility and precision. The integration of Artificial Intelligence (AI), the Internet of Things (IoT), and blockchain into this process isn't just an addition; it's a multiplication of possibilities, each technology bringing its unique strengths to the table.

Artificial Intelligence, for instance, transforms raw data into insights with speed and accuracy that human analysis cannot match. Imagine a healthcare provider using AI to sift through millions of patient records, identifying patterns that lead to a breakthrough in preventive care. This isn't just data analysis; it's innovation at lightning speed.

Meanwhile, the IoT connects the physical and digital worlds in ways previously unimaginable. Sensors in retail stores that track customer movements and preferences can revolutionize the shopping experience, creating a personalized journey for every visitor. This isn't merely tracking; it's a redefinition of customer engagement.

LEADERSHIP IN THE AGE OF DATA: HARNESSING INFORMATION FOR STRATEGIC ADVANTAGE

Blockchain, with its promise of security and transparency, offers a foundation on which trust can be built. Consider the supply chain transparency it can provide, enabling consumers to trace the journey of their purchased products from source to store. This isn't just tracking; it's building trust through transparency.

However, the path to harnessing these technologies for strategic advantage is fraught with challenges. The sheer volume of data can overwhelm, the pace of technological change can intimidate, and the skills gap can hinder progress. Yet, within these challenges lie immense opportunities.

One significant opportunity is the democratization of technology. As digital tools become more user-friendly and accessible, a wider range of people can participate in the digital economy. Small businesses, previously sidelined by the high cost of technology, can now compete on a larger stage, leveraging data analytics to carve out their niche.

Another opportunity is the potential for innovation that these challenges inspire. Necessity breeds invention, and as organizations grapple with data deluge and technological upheaval, they're forced to innovate not just in their products and services but in their very approach to business.

But what does this mean for leaders in the age of data? It calls for a reevaluation of leadership styles, an embrace of continuous learning, and an unwavering focus on flexibility and adaptability. Leaders must become champions of change, encouraging their teams to experiment, learn from failures, and continuously seek improvement.

Moreover, ethical considerations around data usage and privacy have come to the forefront. Leaders are now tasked with navigating the delicate balance between leveraging data for strategic advantage and respecting individual privacy rights. This is not just a legal obligation; it's a moral imperative that can define a company's reputation.

In embracing these challenges and opportunities, organizations must also recognize the importance of a strong data culture. A culture that values data-driven decision making, encourages curiosity, and fosters an environment of transparency and trust. This isn't just about having the right tools; it's about cultivating the right mindset.

So, as we stand at the intersection of data analytics and digital transformation, we face a landscape brimming with potential. Yes, the challenges are significant, but the opportunities for those willing to navigate this complex terrain are boundless.

And so, we return to a fundamental question: How will you leverage the power of data analytics to drive your digital transformation journey? Will you view the challenges as insurmountable obstacles or as stepping stones towards innovation?

This journey of transformation is not for the faint-hearted. It requires courage, curiosity, and an unwavering commitment to innovation. But for those who dare to embark on this journey, the rewards can be monumental, reshaping industries and redefining what it means to be a leader in the age of data.

Remember, in the end, digital transformation isn't just about technology; it's about envisioning a new future and using the tools at our disposal to turn that vision into reality. And at the heart of this endeavor lies the strategic use of data analytics, a powerful ally in our quest for innovation and growth.

Are you ready to harness the power of data for strategic advantage? The journey begins now.

Case Studies: Companies That Have Innovated With Data

In the evolving landscape of global commerce, a select few companies have not just navigated the stormy seas of change; they have harnessed the winds to their advantage. Through innovative uses of data analytics, these trailblazers have redefined their industries, setting new standards for success. Let's delve into the stories of these pioneering firms, examining their strategies, the obstacles they overcame, and the profound impact of their journeys on both market position and financial performance.

In the realm of digital music, Spotify stands out not merely as a streaming service but as a maestro of data-driven personalization. With over 345 million active users, the question looms: how does Spotify ensure each user feels their listening experience is uniquely theirs?

The answer lies in their sophisticated use of data analytics. Spotify's algorithms analyze your listening habits, comparing them with the vast ocean of music and podcast content in their library. But, the innovation doesn't stop at mere recommendations. Have you ever wondered how Spotify's Discover Weekly playlist seems to understand your musical taste so intimately? It's a symphony of collaborative filtering, natural language processing, and audio analysis, all working in concert to predict what you'll love next.

Spotify faced significant challenges, including the massive scale of data processing required for personalized experiences and concerns around user privacy. Yet, by continuously refining their algorithms and maintaining a transparent dialogue with their users about data use, Spotify has not only navigated these challenges but has also enhanced its market position. The result? A platform where every user's experience is as unique as their own fingerprint, driving Spotify's financial performance to new highs.

Imagine the challenge of keeping millions glued to their screens in an era where attention is the most coveted currency. Netflix, the streaming giant, turned to data analytics to script its unprecedented success story.

Netflix's recommendation engine is the unsung hero, powered by a sophisticated understanding of viewer preferences. This engine analyzes billions of hours of watched content to suggest shows and movies you're likely to enjoy. But the innovation doesn't end there. Netflix uses data analytics not just to recommend content but to create it. Shows like "House of

Cards" and "Stranger Things" were greenlit based on insights gleaned from data about viewer preferences, a gamble that paid off handsomely, transforming Netflix from a content distributor to an acclaimed content creator.

The challenges were manifold, from the ethical dilemmas of using viewer data to the technical hurdles of processing and analyzing vast datasets. However, by prioritizing user privacy and investing in cutting-edge technology, Netflix turned these challenges into opportunities, revolutionizing the entertainment industry and significantly boosting its financial outcomes.

In the fast-paced world of fashion, Zara, a flagship brand of the Inditex Group, has outshone its competitors by turning the fast-fashion model on its head. The secret? A relentless focus on fast data.

Zara's approach to data analytics involves tracking customer preferences in real-time, from the styles they browse online to the items they try on in-store. This immediate feedback loop allows Zara to adjust its inventory and designs swiftly, ensuring they always hit the mark with consumer trends.

But the journey wasn't without its thorns. Managing the logistics of rapid production cycles and ensuring the timely analysis of data from multiple sources presented significant challenges. Zara's solution was to invest heavily in its IT infrastructure and foster a culture that values agility and responsiveness.

This strategic use of data analytics has not only cemented Zara's position as a leader in fast fashion but has also translated into robust financial health, with the brand consistently outperforming its competitors in both revenue growth and profitability.

Tesla, the electric vehicle and clean energy company, has not just entered the automotive industry; it has reinvented it, with data analytics steering the wheel of innovation.

Tesla's vehicles, often described as computers on wheels, collect vast amounts of data, from driving patterns to vehicle performance metrics. This data isn't just fodder for analysis; it's the backbone of Tesla's continuous improvement philosophy. Through over-the-air software updates, Tesla uses insights derived from data to enhance vehicle performance, introduce new features, and even improve safety standards, all without the vehicle ever visiting a service center.

Navigating the ethical considerations of data collection and user privacy, alongside the technical challenges of data analysis and software development, required a delicate balancing act. Yet, Tesla's commitment to innovation and its transparent communication with customers have turned potential obstacles into stepping stones toward unprecedented success in the electric vehicle market.

Tesla's data-driven approach has not only propelled it to the forefront of the automotive industry but has also significantly impacted its financial metrics, with market valuation and sales figures that defy traditional industry logic.

The stories of Spotify, Netflix, Zara, and Tesla illuminate the transformative power of data analytics. These companies, each in their distinct industries, have leveraged data not just as a tool for decision-making but as a foundation for innovation, redefining market norms and setting new benchmarks for financial performance.

What these case studies underscore is a universal truth in the age of data: the companies that innovate with data at their core are the ones that lead. They turn challenges into opportunities, navigating the complexities of the modern market with agility and foresight.

The question that now stands before us is not whether data analytics will shape the future of business—it undoubtedly will. The question is, how will you harness the power of data to write your own success story? Will you be a bystander in this era of data-driven transformation, or will you seize the helm, steering your company toward uncharted territories of innovation and growth?

The age of data is here. The time to act is now.

Building a Culture of Data-Driven Experimentation

In the ever-evolving landscape of the digital age, where information flows as freely as water in a river, the concept of leadership has undergone a seismic shift. The leaders of today and tomorrow face a daunting challenge yet an exhilarating opportunity: to harness the torrent of data for strategic advantage. At the heart of this transformation lies the imperative to build a culture of data-driven experimentation. This chapter delves into the intricacies of fostering an environment where data is not just a tool but the bedrock of decision-making, innovation, and strategic foresight.

Central to the ethos of a data-driven organization is the democratization of data. Imagine a realm where data flows unhindered, accessible to all, irrespective of hierarchy or role. In such a world, innovation is not the monopoly of the few but the collective responsibility of the many. How, then, can leaders unlock this potential?

The journey begins with transparency. By making data accessible, leaders empower their teams to ask questions, seek answers, and challenge assumptions. Yet, access alone is not enough. Equipping teams with the tools and skills to analyze and interpret data is equally crucial. This dual approach not only democratizes data but also fosters a sense of ownership and accountability.

But why stop there? Encouraging teams to share insights and learnings across silos ignites a spark of collective curiosity. It's a spark that, when nurtured, transforms into a blazing fire of innovation.

In the heart of a data-driven culture lies the spirit of inquiry. Asking "What if?" is not just encouraged; it's celebrated. But how do leaders cultivate this mindset?

It begins with framing experimentation as a journey of discovery, not a hunt for immediate successes. Encouraging teams to test hypotheses, with data as their guide, embarks them on this journey. Each hypothesis becomes a stepping stone, leading to new insights, whether it confirms an assumption or challenges it.

Leaders play a pivotal role in this process. By setting expectations that not every experiment will yield positive results, they foster an environment where failure is not a stigma but a badge of courage. It's a subtle shift in perspective that has profound implications for innovation.

Innovation thrives in diversity. The fusion of different perspectives, expertise, and experiences creates a fertile ground for groundbreaking ideas. Cross-functional data teams embody this principle.

By bringing together individuals from various departments, these teams break down the invisible walls that silos create. Marketing experts, IT professionals, customer service representatives, and others, all seated at the same table, united by a common goal: to leverage data in solving complex problems.

This collaborative approach not only broadens the scope of experimentation but also accelerates the pace of innovation. Ideas, once confined to the narrow corridors of departments, now flow freely, enriching the collective intelligence of the organization.

The path of experimentation is fraught with failures. Yet, within each failure lies a lesson waiting to be uncovered.

Embracing a fail-fast approach is not about celebrating failure but about learning from it rapidly and efficiently.

This mindset shift requires leaders to redefine success. Success is no longer just achieving the desired outcome but also gaining insights that refine future strategies. It's a perspective that views each experiment, regardless of its outcome, as a valuable piece of the puzzle.

Leaders can cultivate this mindset by celebrating the learnings from failed experiments. Sharing stories of what didn't work, and more importantly, why, becomes as important as celebrating successes. It's a practice that not only demystifies failure but also embeds a culture of continuous learning.

In the age of data, the leaders who dare to foster a culture of data-driven experimentation are the ones who will navigate their organizations towards uncharted territories of growth and innovation. It's a journey that demands courage, curiosity, and an unwavering commitment to learning.

But remember, building this culture is not a destination but a continuous journey. It's a journey marked by the democratization of data, the courage to question, the wisdom to learn from failure, and the collaborative spirit of cross-functional teams.

The question that stands before you, as a leader in the age of data, is not whether you will embark on this journey—but how far and how fast you will travel.

The age of data beckons. Let the journey begin.

Cultivating a Data-Driven Culture

Characteristics of a Data-Driven Organizational Culture

In the vast expanse of today's business landscapes, a new titan strides with confidence, its footsteps reverberating with the crunch of binary codes and the whisper of data streams. This titan, known as the data-driven organizational culture, thrives on the pillars of curiosity, openness to change, and an unwavering commitment to harnessing data for strategic decision-making. But what are the intricacies of these characteristics, and how do they coalesce to form an invincible architecture of efficiency, innovation, and competitive advantage?

Curiosity, the spark that ignites the flame of knowledge, stands at the forefront of this cultural paradigm. Imagine a room filled with the brightest minds, eyes alight with the fervor of discovery, each question they pose a stepping stone towards uncharted territories of insight and understanding. In such a culture, questions are welcomed, no matter how trivial they may seem. "What if?" becomes the mantra, a powerful incantation that opens doorways to transformational strategies and groundbreaking products. This relentless pursuit of knowledge not only fuels innovation but also fosters an environment where learning and growth are intrinsic values.

Transitioning from the zeal of curiosity, the narrative flows seamlessly into the realm of openness to change. Here, adaptability is not just a skill but a cherished value. Picture a mighty river, its waters eternally flowing, adapting to the contours of the land, sometimes a gentle stream, other times a roaring torrent. Similarly, a data-driven organization embraces change with grace, understanding that in the fluidity of market dynamics, flexibility is synonymous with survival. This openness is not without its challenges; it requires dismantling the fortresses of the status quo, encouraging a mindset where change is not an adversary but an ally in the quest for excellence.

At the heart of this culture beats a commitment to using data in decision-making processes. Decisions, once guided by intuition and experience alone, now stand on the solid ground of empirical evidence. Imagine a bridge spanning the chasm of uncertainty, each plank a piece of analyzed data, offering a safe passage to informed choices. In such an environment, data is not just numbers and graphs; it is a language, a means of communication that transcends personal biases and assumptions. This commitment transforms the decision-making process into a transparent, objective, and logical course of action, ensuring that strategies are not just good but optimal.

The benefits of fostering a data-driven culture are manifold. Efficiency, for one, sees a significant uptick. Processes that once meandered in the labyrinth of trial and error now follow a direct path illuminated by data. This streamlined approach not only saves time but also resources, leading to a leaner, more agile organization.

LEADERSHIP IN THE AGE OF DATA: HARNESSING INFORMATION FOR STRATEGIC ADVANTAGE

Innovation, too, finds fertile ground in this culture. With data as the muse, creativity transcends conventional boundaries, giving birth to solutions and products that often defy expectations. This relentless innovation not only keeps the organization ahead of the curve but also cements its position as a leader in the market.

But perhaps the most coveted advantage is the competitive edge that a data-driven culture bestows. In a world where information is the currency of power, having a strategic approach to data is akin to possessing a map in a treasure hunt. It allows organizations to anticipate trends, understand customer needs on a granular level, and make strategic moves with confidence and precision.

Yet, the journey to cultivating such a culture is not devoid of obstacles. It demands a paradigm shift, a willingness to venture into the unknown, and a steadfast commitment to a vision that places data at the heart of every endeavor.

Is your organization ready to embrace this transformation?

The road ahead is challenging, no doubt, but the rewards are unparalleled. For those who dare to walk this path, the future is not just bright; it is illuminated by the clear, unerring light of data.

In conclusion, a data-driven organizational culture is not merely an option in the age of information; it is a necessity. It is the bedrock upon which the future of strategic advantage is built, a culture that champions curiosity, embraces change, and elevates decision-making to an art form guided by the insights gleaned from data. As we forge ahead in this era of digital transformation, let us remember that data is not just a tool but a compass, guiding us towards a horizon brimming with potential and promise.

Leadership Strategies for Promoting Data-Centric Thinking

In the quest to champion a data-centric culture, leadership plays a pivotal role. The journey toward embedding data at the heart of an organization's ethos begins with those at the helm. Leaders must not only preach the virtues of data-driven decision-making but also embody these principles in their actions, decisions, and strategies.

Leading by Example: The Beacon of Change

A leader's actions set the tone for the organization's culture. Consider the CEO who, before making any strategic decision, asks for data analyses and projections. This leader attends meetings not just with a vision but with insights gleaned from data. Such behavior sends a powerful message: data is not optional; it is essential.

Imagine a scenario where, during a high-stakes meeting, instead of relying solely on gut feelings or past experiences, a leader asks, "What does the data tell us?" This simple question can have a profound impact. It encourages a mindset shift across all levels of the organization, fostering an environment where data becomes the common language of decision-making.

Providing Data Literacy Training: Empowering Teams

LEADERSHIP IN THE AGE OF DATA: HARNESSING INFORMATION FOR STRATEGIC ADVANTAGE

Knowledge is power, and in the age of data, this adage holds truer than ever. However, data literacy is not innate; it must be cultivated. Recognizing this, effective leaders invest in comprehensive data literacy programs for their teams.

Picture a series of workshops where employees from various departments learn not just to analyze data but to question it, to see beyond the numbers to the stories they tell. Such training demystifies data, making it accessible and, more importantly, actionable for everyone, regardless of their role.

Encouraging Data Exploration and Sharing: The Collaborative Spirit

Curiosity drives innovation, and in a data-centric organization, leaders encourage an exploratory approach to data. They foster an environment where team members feel empowered to dive into data, uncover insights, and share their findings.

Imagine a digital dashboard accessible to all, where employees can post questions, share data visualizations, and collaborate on projects. This not only democratizes data but also cultivates a sense of ownership and pride in data-driven achievements.

Recognizing and Rewarding Data-Driven Achievements: The Motivational Force

Recognition is a powerful motivator. Leaders who celebrate data-driven successes, no matter how small, reinforce the value of a data-centric approach. Consider an award for the "Data Innovation of the Month," given to teams or individuals who have used data in creative ways to solve problems or improve processes. Such recognition not only motivates but also inspires others to think critically about how they can leverage data in their work.

The Challenges Ahead

Shifting to a data-centric mindset is not without its challenges. Resistance to change, data silos, and a lack of data literacy can hinder progress. However, with persistent effort, clear communication, and unwavering commitment, leaders can overcome these obstacles. They can transform their organizations into data-driven entities, ready to navigate the complexities of the modern business landscape.

In conclusion, the role of leadership in promoting data-centric thinking cannot be overstated. Leaders must lead by example, provide the tools and training necessary for their teams to succeed, encourage exploration and collaboration, and recognize achievements in the realm of data.

The future belongs to those who understand and leverage the power of data. The question now is, will you be among the leaders who guide their organizations into this new dawn of strategic advantage?

Your journey starts today. Embrace it.

Overcoming Resistance and Fostering Buy-in

Embarking on the journey toward a data-driven culture is akin to steering a ship through uncharted waters. The path is fraught with obstacles, chief among them being resistance from team members and a lack of trust in data analytics. Such hurdles, however, are not insurmountable. Through clear communication, the demonstration of data's value via quick wins, and engaging team members in the transformation process, leaders can navigate these challenges effectively.

Why do individuals resist the shift to a data-centric approach? At the heart of resistance often lies fear—fear of the unknown, fear of obsolescence, and, fundamentally, fear of failure. The digital dashboard, once a source of curiosity, becomes a symbol of apprehension. "Will I be able to adapt?" one might wonder, staring at a screen filled with numbers.

To dismantle these fears, start with clear communication. Transparency is key. Articulate not only the what and the how but, most importantly, the why. Why is the shift to a data-driven culture crucial for the organization's future? How will it benefit each team member, not just the company? Answers to these questions can demystify the process and align personal and organizational goals.

Imagine the impact of sharing a success story in an all-hands meeting where a data-driven decision led to a significant win for the company. Picture the scene – the room's energy shifts as the story unfolds, skepticism giving way to intrigue. Suddenly, the data doesn't seem so daunting anymore. It's a tool, a means to an end that everyone can wield with the right training and mindset.

Securing quick wins is another potent strategy. Identify opportunities where data analytics can lead to immediate improvements. Perhaps it's optimizing marketing campaigns or streamlining supply chain logistics. When team members see tangible benefits—increased sales, reduced costs, happier customers—their faith in data's power grows.

Let's not overlook the importance of engaging team members in the data transformation process. This engagement can take many forms, from participating in data literacy training to contributing ideas for data-driven projects. Consider creating a "data sandbox," a safe space where employees can experiment with data, make mistakes, and learn without fear of repercussions. Such initiatives not only build proficiency but also foster a sense of ownership and pride in the data-driven journey.

Involvement breeds commitment. When Jane, a long-time employee skeptical of the new data initiative, sees her suggestion for improving customer data collection implemented and yielding positive results, her perspective shifts. She becomes a champion of the cause, sharing her experience and encouraging her peers to get involved.

What about the role of leaders in this transformative journey? Leaders must be the beacon of change, consistently demonstrating their commitment to a data-driven culture. This might mean openly discussing their decisions based on data analytics, acknowledging the challenges, and celebrating the milestones, no matter how small.

LEADERSHIP IN THE AGE OF DATA: HARNESSING INFORMATION FOR STRATEGIC ADVANTAGE

Leaders should also be accessible, offering an open door to anyone with concerns or suggestions about the data transformation process. When Mike, a team leader, expresses his team's frustration with a new data tool, a leader's willingness to listen and address the issue not only resolves the immediate problem but also strengthens trust in the leadership's commitment to the data-driven shift.

Incorporating quotations or dialogues can add depth to the narrative. For example, a leader might share a quote that resonates with the data-driven mission: "In God we trust; all others must bring data." - W. Edwards Deming. This simple statement underscores the importance of data in decision-making and can serve as a rallying cry for the organization.

Ultimately, the shift to a data-driven culture is a journey, not a sprint. It requires patience, persistence, and a willingness to adapt. By overcoming resistance and fostering buy-in through clear communication, quick wins, and active engagement, leaders can harness the power of information for strategic advantage.

The transformation is challenging, yes, but the rewards are innumerable. A data-driven organization is not only more efficient and competitive but also better positioned to navigate the complexities of the modern business landscape.

The question is no longer if you should embark on this journey but how quickly you can set sail. The age of data awaits, and the time to act is now. Will you lead the charge?

Measuring and Incentivizing Data-Driven Performance

In the relentless pursuit of fostering a data-driven culture, the measure of success extends beyond the initial implementation of data analytics tools and strategies. It delves into the heart of how effectively these initiatives are woven into the very fabric of organizational operations and mindset. How, then, can leaders quantify this success and, more importantly, incentivize the behaviors that drive it? This chapter aims to unravel these complexities, offering a roadmap to measure and galvanize data-driven performance.

Before embarking on the journey of incentivization, one must first establish robust metrics for measuring data-driven success. These metrics should not only reflect quantitative outcomes, such as increased revenue or optimized operational efficiency but also qualitative aspects like enhanced decision-making agility and improved team collaboration.

Imagine a scenario where a marketing team leverages data analytics to refine their customer segmentation. The success of this initiative could be measured by a tangible uptick in engagement rates. Yet, equally important is the team's enhanced ability to make informed decisions swiftly, a qualitative shift that breeds a more dynamic, responsive marketing strategy.

In crafting these metrics, leaders should adhere to the SMART criteria—ensuring each is Specific, Measurable, Achievable, Relevant, and Time-bound. An effective metric, for instance, could be the reduction of decision-making time by 30% within six months, attributable directly to data-driven insights.

With the yardstick of success in place, the focus shifts to incentivization—a catalyst for engraining data-driven behaviors within an organization's ethos. Incentives, however, should extend beyond mere financial rewards. They ought to encapsulate recognition programs, career development opportunities, and performance-based rewards, all tailored to foster a culture where data is king.

Recognition programs serve as a powerful tool in this arsenal. Consider the impact of a 'Data Champion of the Month' award, spotlighting individuals or teams who have notably leveraged data to drive decision-making or innovation. This not only elevates the status of data-driven initiatives but also nurtures a sense of pride and achievement among staff.

Career development opportunities further sweeten the pot. Employees who demonstrate a keen aptitude for data analytics could be offered specialized training, certifications, or roles that position them as data evangelists within the organization. Such opportunities not only incentivize individuals to hone their data literacy but also underscore the organization's commitment to nurturing its talent pool in alignment with its strategic objectives.

Performance-based rewards, when strategically deployed, can also play a pivotal role. Imagine tying a portion of bonus structures to the achievement of data-driven objectives. This tangible link between data-centric behaviors and financial rewards can significantly motivate teams to embrace and champion data analytics in their daily operations.

Measurement and incentivization are not merely steps in a process.

They are the lifeblood of sustaining a data-driven culture.

How, then, can you, as a leader, implement these strategies within your own teams? Have you identified the metrics that truly encapsulate success in your context? Are the incentives you're considering genuinely aligned with fostering a culture that prizes data-driven decision-making?

Implementing these strategies requires a delicate balance. It's a dance between celebrating short-term wins and keeping an eye on the long-term vision. Leaders must continuously iterate on the metrics and incentives, ensuring they remain relevant and compelling as the organization evolves. It's about striking that perfect cadence that keeps the organization in lockstep with the dynamic nature of data and its infinite possibilities.

"Seeing my team's project highlighted as a benchmark for data-driven success was a game-changer," recalls Maria, a project manager. "It wasn't just about the recognition. It was a moment that underscored the transformative power of data in our work."

At its core, the aim is simple. Cultivate a culture where data-driven decision-making becomes second nature. Where every team member, from the CEO to the front-line employee, instinctively turns to data as the compass guiding their actions.

LEADERSHIP IN THE AGE OF DATA: HARNESSING INFORMATION FOR STRATEGIC ADVANTAGE

The journey towards a data-driven culture is both challenging and exhilarating. As leaders, the responsibility lies with us to not only chart the course but also ensure our crew is motivated, equipped, and recognized as we navigate these waters. By adeptly measuring and incentivizing data-driven performance, we not only accelerate our voyage into the age of data but also unlock the strategic advantage buried within the numbers. The time to act is now. Are you ready to lead your team into the future?

Data-Driven Strategic Planning

Role of Data in Identifying Market Trends and Customer Needs

In the labyrinth of modern commerce, data stands as the North Star for organizations navigating the murky waters of market trends and customer needs. This chapter delves deep into the transformative power of data analytics, a beacon that illuminates the path to understanding and anticipating the ever-evolving desires of consumers and the unpredictable shifts in market dynamics.

Imagine walking through a bustling market, each stall brimming with insights and opportunities, hidden amidst the cacophony of the crowd. This is the marketplace of today—vast, vibrant, and echoing with the voices of millions of customers. But how does one listen to these whispers and shouts, distinguishing fleeting fancies from lasting desires? The answer lies in harnessing the prowess of data analytics.

At the heart of this exploration is sentiment analysis, a sophisticated technique that parses through the vast expanse of data generated by online interactions, customer reviews, and social media engagements. Picture a tool so discerning it can sift through the nuances of language, identifying not just the content but the context and emotion behind every word. This is sentiment analysis in action, a key that unlocks the door to understanding how customers feel about products, services, and brands. It's like having a direct line to the collective consciousness of the market, offering insights that are as invaluable as they are intricate.

But sentiment analysis is just the beginning. Enter trend forecasting, a discipline that combines the art of intuition with the science of data. Through the analysis of historical data patterns, trend forecasting projects the trajectory of market movements, anticipating shifts before they occur. Armed with this foresight, businesses can pivot with agility, aligning their strategies to ride the wave of emerging trends rather than being caught in their undertow. Imagine being able to predict the next big thing in fashion, technology, or consumer behavior. This is the power of trend forecasting, a lighthouse guiding ships through the fog of uncertainty.

Equally critical to the strategic arsenal is customer segmentation. This technique divides the vast ocean of consumers into manageable streams, grouping individuals based on shared characteristics, behaviors, and preferences. Such segmentation allows for personalized marketing strategies that speak directly to the heart of each group's desires, creating a sense of connection and understanding. It's akin to a craftsman tailoring a garment to fit the unique contours of each client, ensuring not just satisfaction but delight.

But how does one translate these analytical insights into tangible strategies? It begins with asking the right questions. What do our customers truly want? How can we serve them better? Where are we missing the mark? Data analytics offers not just answers but a roadmap to innovation and improvement.

Consider, for instance, the power of one-line paragraphs in storytelling.

Impactful.

They serve as a pause in the narrative, a moment for the reader to reflect and absorb. Similarly, in analyzing data, sometimes it's a single insight that can change the course of a strategy, illuminating opportunities that were previously hidden in plain sight.

Throughout this exploration, the importance of simplicity cannot be overstated. In a world awash with data, the ability to distill complex information into clear, actionable insights is akin to finding water in the desert. It's not the quantity of data that matters but the quality of the insights derived from it.

To breathe life into these concepts, let's consider the story of a small, family-owned bakery that used data analytics to transform its business. By analyzing customer reviews and social media engagement, they discovered a growing demand for gluten-free options—a trend they had previously overlooked. This insight led them to revamp their menu, introducing a range of gluten-free pastries that catapulted them to local fame. Their secret? Listening to the data.

In the words of a renowned business strategist, "Data is the flashlight in the darkness of uncertainty." This chapter aims to be that flashlight, guiding readers through the intricacies of data analytics and its application in identifying market trends and customer needs.

LEADERSHIP IN THE AGE OF DATA: HARNESSING INFORMATION FOR STRATEGIC ADVANTAGE

As we conclude this exploration, remember that the landscape of commerce is ever-changing, with new challenges and opportunities emerging at the speed of thought. In this age of data, the ability to adapt, innovate, and anticipate is not just a strategic advantage but a necessity.

Data is not just numbers and charts; it's the voice of the market, the pulse of consumer desires. And in this age of information, those who listen closely will not only survive but thrive.

Utilizing Data Analytics for Competitive Analysis

In an era brimming with information, the strategic utilization of data analytics transcends mere understanding of consumer behavior, venturing boldly into the realm of competitive analysis. This chapter embarks on a journey through the intricate landscape of leveraging data analytics to dissect and understand competitors' strategies, market positioning, and overall performance. By doing so, businesses can sculpt a strategic advantage that is both resilient and dynamic.

Ever wondered how giants of industry manage to stay steps ahead of their competition? The answer often lies hidden within the troves of data they collect and analyze. Competitive analysis through data analytics isn't just about observing what your rivals are doing; it's about peering into the future, predicting their next moves, and preparing to counteract with precision.

To begin, envision a chessboard. Each piece has a role, a purpose, and a potential path to victory. In the grand scheme of competitive analysis, data serves as the eyes that see beyond the immediate moves, anticipating strategies and endgames. But how does one transform raw data into a coherent strategy that provides this level of insight?

The first step lies in monitoring. Observing competitors' online presence, from their social media interactions to customer reviews, can unveil a wealth of insights. Sophisticated algorithms and machine learning can help filter through the noise, identifying patterns and shifts in sentiment that signal changes in strategy or highlight areas of weakness. This digital sleuthing, when done correctly, paints a vivid picture of a competitor's performance and the effectiveness of their market positioning.

But monitoring is only the tip of the iceberg. Delving deeper requires a keen understanding of market positioning. How do competitors align themselves within the market ecosystem? What unique value propositions do they offer, and how are these perceived by the target audience? Data analytics can uncover the answers to these questions, offering a bird's eye view of the competitive landscape. By mapping out competitors' positions, a business can identify gaps in the market—opportunities for differentiation that can be exploited for strategic advantage.

Performance analysis further complements this approach. By examining competitors' sales data, customer retention rates, and even employee satisfaction, businesses can gauge the health

LEADERSHIP IN THE AGE OF DATA: HARNESSING INFORMATION FOR STRATEGIC ADVANTAGE

and potential vulnerabilities of their rivals. Such analysis requires a judicious blend of external data and internal metrics, comparing and contrasting to identify areas of strength and opportunities for improvement.

Imagine, for a moment, a scenario where a company uncovers through data analytics that a competitor's recent product launch is underperforming due to poor customer satisfaction. Armed with this knowledge, the company can strategically highlight the superior aspects of their own product, potentially capturing a portion of the disillusioned customer base.

Now, consider the role of direct questions in engaging with this data-driven strategy. What specific aspects of our competitor's strategy are yielding results? Where are they failing to connect with their audience? Questions like these spur deeper analysis and encourage a more nuanced approach to competitive strategy.

A striking example of this analytical approach in action can be seen in the story of a tech startup that utilized data analytics to track the patent filings of its main competitors. By understanding the types of innovations their competitors were investing in, the startup was able to pivot its research and development focus, ultimately leading to the creation of a groundbreaking new product that captured significant market share.

"In the modern battlefield of business, information is ammunition," remarked a leading industry expert. This statement underscores the essence of competitive analysis through data analytics. It's about arming oneself with the knowledge to make informed decisions, anticipate the moves of competitors, and craft strategies that ensure sustainable growth and success.

To encapsulate, the power of data analytics in competitive analysis cannot be overstated. It transforms invisible patterns into tangible insights, guiding businesses through the labyrinth of market dynamics and competitor strategies. The key lies in the meticulous collection, analysis, and application of data to inform strategic decisions that propel a business forward.

As this chapter closes, remember that the landscape of competition is perpetually shifting. In the age of data, the ability to adapt, foresee, and innovate is the cornerstone of strategic advantage. The future belongs to those who not only gather information but harness it with precision and creativity to stay one leap ahead in the game of business.

Frameworks for Data-Informed Strategic Planning

In the labyrinthine corridors of business where uncertainty looms at every corner, leaders are constantly seeking the guiding light of clarity. This clarity, more often than not, is illuminated by the strategic use of data. Yet, the mere collection of data is akin to gathering raw ore from the earth's depths; its true value is unlocked only through refinement and careful application. The question then becomes, how can leaders harness this raw data for strategic planning that aligns with organizational objectives? The answer lies in the adoption of robust frameworks and tools designed for this very purpose.

Embarking on the journey of data-informed strategic planning requires a foundational understanding of the frameworks that serve as the scaffolding for this process. One such cornerstone is the Balanced Scorecard (BSC) framework. Picture, if you will, a bridge spanning the chasm between strategy and execution. The BSC acts as this bridge, enabling organizations to translate their vision and strategy into actionable objectives across four perspectives: Financial, Customer, Internal Process, and Learning and Growth.

Through the lens of the BSC, leaders can weave data into each perspective, setting measurable targets and identifying the key performance indicators (KPIs) that will signal progress. Imagine a manufacturing company aiming to increase market share. By applying the BSC, it might identify customer satisfaction scores as a critical KPI within the Customer Perspective, guiding strategic initiatives focused on quality improvement and customer engagement.

As vital as frameworks like the BSC are, the toolset for data-informed strategic planning also includes methodologies that enhance decision-making capabilities. Among these, SWOT Analysis (Strengths, Weaknesses, Opportunities, Threats) stands out for its simplicity and effectiveness. With roots reaching back to the strategic planning practices of the 1960s, SWOT Analysis remains a powerful tool for leaders to align their strategies with both internal capabilities and external market conditions.

Imagine conducting a SWOT Analysis in the context of a rapidly evolving technology sector. A tech firm might uncover, through rigorous data analysis, an opportunity in the form of an emerging market trend that aligns with its core strengths, such as superior product innovation. Conversely, the same analysis might highlight a significant threat from a new competitor's disruptive technology. Such insights become the bedrock upon which strategic plans are built, ensuring they are both responsive to external dynamics and grounded in the organization's inherent strengths and weaknesses.

Yet, data-informed strategic planning is not solely about the frameworks and tools; it's also about the mindset. Leaders must cultivate a culture of curiosity, where questions like "What does this data tell us about our customers' evolving needs?" or "How can we turn this emerging trend to our advantage?" are part of everyday strategic discussions.

In this age of data, the strategic planning process is akin to navigating a ship through foggy waters. Frameworks like the BSC and tools like SWOT Analysis serve as the compass and map, guiding the journey. However, it's the skillful captain—the data-informed leader—who steers the ship safely to its destination.

Consider a real-world application of these principles. A retail chain, armed with customer data, identifies a shift towards online shopping. By integrating this insight into its strategic planning through the use of the BSC, the company reallocates resources to enhance its e-commerce platform, tailoring the online shopping experience to customer preferences unearthed in the data. As a result, the retail chain not only retains its market position but also expands its customer base, showcasing the tangible benefits of a data-informed approach.

But let us not forget, the journey of strategic planning is perpetual, with the landscape continually evolving. In this dynamic environment, the most successful organizations are those that remain agile, their strategies informed by a constant stream of data, analyzed through the prism of tried and tested frameworks and tools.

In closing, the path to leadership in the age of data is marked by the strategic harnessing of information. It is a path that demands not only the right tools and frameworks but also a mindset attuned to the possibilities hidden within data. As we forge ahead, let us hold fast to the principle that in the vast sea of information, strategic advantage lies in knowing not just how to navigate, but where to look. The future of leadership belongs to those who, guided by data, can envision a course not just for survival, but for prosperity.

Aligning Data Strategy With Organizational Goals

In the ever-evolving tapestry of the business world, aligning data strategy with organizational goals emerges as a pivotal chapter in the narrative of success. This alignment, however, is not a mere act of balancing figures and charts; it is an artful dance between insight and action, orchestrated by leaders who understand the profound impact of data on strategic advantage.

Imagine a symphony, where each musician's contribution is critical to the harmony of the whole. In much the same way, every data initiative within an organization contributes to the overarching goal of strategic success. The conductor of this symphony is the visionary leader who sees beyond the horizon, recognizing that data is not just numbers but a beacon guiding the organization's journey.

But how do leaders champion data-driven strategies effectively? And what does it mean to foster cross-functional collaboration in this context? These questions mark the beginning of our exploration into aligning data strategy with organizational goals.

First and foremost, leaders must embody the principle of leading by example. Championing a data-driven strategy begins with a commitment to data literacy at all levels of leadership. It involves demystifying data, making it accessible, and encouraging curiosity. A leader's engagement with data sets a tone, signaling its value to the entire organization.

Diving deeper, the integration of data initiatives with organizational goals necessitates a clear vision. This vision should articulate not only the desired outcome but also the role of data in achieving it. For instance, if the goal is to enhance customer satisfaction, the leader's vision might involve leveraging customer feedback data to inform service improvements. By articulating this vision, leaders provide a compass that guides data initiatives, ensuring they remain aligned with organizational objectives.

LEADERSHIP IN THE AGE OF DATA: HARNESSING INFORMATION FOR STRATEGIC ADVANTAGE

Cross-functional collaboration is the bridge connecting data strategy with organizational goals. It is the acknowledgment that data does not belong to a silo but is a cross-cutting asset that can inform decisions across departments. But how can leaders foster this collaboration?

Creating cross-functional teams dedicated to specific data initiatives is a start. These teams bring together diverse perspectives, enabling a more holistic approach to data analysis and application. Encouraging open communication and shared learning among these teams can further break down silos, fostering a culture where data is seen as a shared resource.

Consider a scenario where a marketing team's data reveals a shift in consumer behavior. By collaborating with the product development team, this insight can inform new product features or adjustments, aligning product strategy with market needs. It is this kind of cross-functional collaboration that turns data into a strategic asset.

Moreover, aligning data strategy with organizational goals requires a framework for measuring success. This involves setting clear metrics that reflect both the data initiatives and the broader organizational objectives. Regularly reviewing these metrics ensures that the data strategy remains on track and provides an opportunity for course correction if needed.

But what happens when data reveals a need for a strategic pivot?

Leaders must be agile, ready to adapt their strategies based on new insights. This agility is a hallmark of a data-informed organization, where decisions are made not on the basis of tradition, but on the evidence presented by data. It requires a willingness to question assumptions and a culture where change is embraced as a pathway to improvement.

In closing, consider the power of a question: "What could we achieve if every decision were informed by data?"

This question invites us to envision a future where data is not just a tool but a compass guiding strategic decisions. It challenges leaders to champion data-driven strategies with a commitment to alignment, collaboration, and agility.

In the age of data, the leaders who embrace this challenge are the ones who will navigate their organizations to new horizons of success. They understand that in the intricate dance between data and strategy, it is the harmonious alignment with organizational goals that ultimately leads to strategic advantage.

And so, the journey continues, with data as our guide and strategic alignment as our destination. Let us embark on this path with a clear vision, a collaborative spirit, and the courage to let data lead the way.

For in the alignment of data strategy with organizational goals lies not just the promise of competitive advantage, but the realization of our fullest potential.

Building and Leading Data-Driven Teams

Assembling Teams With Diverse Data Skills

In the digital era, data reigns supreme. It whispers the secrets of consumer behavior, shouts the patterns in global markets, and sings the possibilities of innovation. But who listens to these varied tunes, interprets their rhythms, and composes strategies that align with their melodies? The answer lies in assembling teams with a diverse set of data skills.

Imagine, if you will, a group of individuals, each with their own unique expertise. Data engineers lay the tracks, data scientists explore the uncharted territories, analysts decipher the codes, and visualization experts paint the stories hidden within numbers. Together, they form an orchestra of insights, harmonizing disparate data points into strategies that propel businesses forward.

Why, then, is the assembly of such a team critical in our age of information?

Diversity in skills translates to a panoramic view of possibilities. Data engineers ensure the flow of data is seamless and secure, providing the foundation upon which insights are built. Without them, the data might as well be a locked treasure chest. Data scientists, with their knack for predictive modeling and machine learning, predict trends and outcomes, turning raw data into valuable forecasts. Analysts scrutinize the data, identifying patterns and anomalies that could indicate opportunities or threats. Lastly, visualization experts transform complex datasets into understandable and actionable visuals, enabling decision-makers to grasp intricate insights at a glance.

The process of recruiting these talented individuals begins with understanding the unique value each brings to the table. Job descriptions must go beyond the traditional, incorporating the need for creativity, curiosity, and collaboration. How does one lure such rare birds? By fostering an environment where innovation thrives and continuous learning is the norm. Interviews should not only assess technical prowess but also the ability to communicate complex ideas simply and work harmoniously in diverse teams.

Once on board, the journey of development and retention takes center stage. Tailored training programs that cater to both the enhancement of technical skills and the soft skills necessary for collaboration can make all the difference. Remember, a chain is only as strong as its weakest link. Regular team-building activities and projects that encourage cross-disciplinary learning can strengthen these links, forging a team that is robust and resilient.

But how does one ensure that this finely tuned ensemble stays together?

Recognition and appreciation play a pivotal role. Public acknowledgment of achievements, opportunities for career advancement, and a culture that values each member's

LEADERSHIP IN THE AGE OF DATA: HARNESSING INFORMATION FOR STRATEGIC ADVANTAGE

contribution can foster loyalty and a sense of belonging. Flexible work arrangements and a focus on work-life balance are not perks but necessities in retaining top talent in this competitive landscape.

Consider the story of DataDreams Inc., a company once struggling to make sense of its vast data lakes. By assembling a diverse data team, they not only unlocked the value hidden within their data but also fostered a culture of innovation that attracted top talent from across the globe. Their secret? A commitment to continuous learning, an environment that celebrated diversity of thought, and a leadership that understood the power of data when wielded by a team with varied skills.

In conclusion, the assembly of diverse data teams is not a luxury but a necessity in the age of data. It demands a strategic approach to recruiting, developing, and retaining individuals with a broad range of data skills. Leaders who embrace this approach will find themselves at the helm of organizations that are not only data-driven but also resilient, innovative, and poised for sustainable growth.

The question then is not whether to build such a team but how quickly you can bring them together. Will you heed the call of the data age and harness the power of diversity in skills for strategic advantage?

The future, rich with data-driven possibilities, awaits your answer.

Fostering Collaboration and Alignment

In the labyrinth of data that characterizes our modern era, the ability to foster collaboration and alignment emerges as a beacon of strategy for leaders seeking to harness information for strategic advantage. This chapter delves deep into the heart of what it means to break down silos, unite departments, and ensure the seamless application of data insights across an organization. The journey is intricate, requiring a nuanced understanding of team dynamics, a commitment to shared goals, and an unwavering focus on the bigger picture.

Picture this: a company where every department operates as an island, isolated by the vast sea of data that surrounds them. Information flows are fragmented, insights are hoarded rather than shared, and the potential for innovation is stifled by the walls of these silos. This is the antithesis of what we strive for in the age of data. The question then arises, how do we dismantle these barriers to foster a culture of collaboration and alignment?

Firstly, leaders must champion the cause of transparency. Envision an environment where data is not just accessible but actively shared across teams and departments. This requires not only the right technological tools but also a cultural shift towards openness and trust. Leaders can set the tone by demonstrating the value of sharing insights and encouraging teams to look beyond their immediate tasks to the broader organizational goals.

LEADERSHIP IN THE AGE OF DATA: HARNESSING INFORMATION FOR STRATEGIC ADVANTAGE

But transparency alone is not enough. The next step involves cultivating cross-functional projects that require the collaboration of diverse teams. Imagine a project that brings together data scientists, marketing professionals, and operations staff, each contributing their unique perspective towards a common goal. Such initiatives not only break down silos but also foster a sense of unity and shared purpose. They serve as fertile ground for innovation, where the fusion of different ideas and approaches can lead to breakthrough solutions.

How, then, can leaders ensure these cross-functional projects thrive? The answer lies in effective communication. It's about creating channels where ideas can be exchanged freely, feedback is given constructively, and every voice is heard. Regular meetings, workshops, and informal gatherings can serve as platforms for this exchange, building bridges between teams and aligning them towards common objectives.

Yet, fostering collaboration goes beyond just bringing people together. It requires alignment on goals, strategies, and metrics. Leaders must articulate a clear vision for what success looks like, ensuring that all team members understand how their contributions fit into the larger picture. This alignment turns a group of individuals into a cohesive team, driven by a shared purpose and mutual accountability.

Consider the impact on a data-driven project when every member, from the data engineer to the marketing analyst, is aligned on the objective, whether it's improving customer satisfaction, streamlining operations, or driving sales. The synergy of their combined efforts can propel the project to new heights, achieving outcomes that far exceed what could be accomplished in isolation.

But what happens when challenges arise, as they inevitably will? This is where the true test of collaboration and alignment lies. Leaders must foster a culture of resilience, where obstacles are seen not as dead-ends but as opportunities for learning and growth. Encouraging a mindset of problem-solving and adaptability ensures that teams can navigate challenges without losing sight of their goals.

In the end, the success of data-driven projects hinges not just on the quality of the data or the sophistication of the analytics but on the ability of people to work together towards a common aim. It's about harnessing the collective intelligence, creativity, and drive of the organization to turn data into a strategic asset.

And so, we return to our guiding question: How do we transform a sea of data into a wellspring of strategic advantage? The answer lies in our ability to foster collaboration and alignment, to tear down the walls that divide us and build bridges that unite us. In doing so, we unlock the full potential of our teams, our data, and our organizations.

The journey is complex, fraught with challenges, and requires a steadfast commitment to the principles of openness, communication, and shared purpose. But for those leaders who are willing to embark on this journey, the rewards are immeasurable. They will find themselves at the helm of organizations that are not just data-driven but also agile, innovative, and poised for enduring success.

Let this be our call to action: to champion collaboration and alignment as the cornerstones of leadership in the age of data. Together, we can turn the tide, transforming the vast oceans of information into a force for strategic advantage.

Encouraging Continuous Learning and Professional Growth

In the ever-evolving landscape of data analytics, where the terrain shifts with each technological advancement and the horizon expands with every dataset uncovered, the imperative for continuous learning and professional growth cannot be overstated. As leaders, the responsibility falls upon us not only to navigate these changes but to ensure our teams are equally equipped for the journey.

Imagine a world where the ceaseless influx of data, rather than overwhelming, becomes a source of endless learning opportunities. In this world, leaders cultivate an environment where curiosity thrives, skills are perpetually honed, and growth is not just encouraged but expected. This chapter delves into how such an environment can be created, focusing on training programs, workshops, conferences, and access to learning resources as the tools at our disposal.

Training programs, meticulously designed and thoughtfully implemented, serve as the backbone of professional development. Leaders must champion these initiatives, ensuring they are both relevant and accessible. Consider a program tailored specifically for data analysts, focusing on the latest machine learning techniques. By investing in such programs, we not only sharpen our team's skills but also signal our commitment to their growth.

Workshops, often more interactive and hands-on, offer a different avenue for development. Picture a session where team members collaboratively tackle real-world data problems, guided by an expert in the field. The benefits of such workshops extend beyond the acquisition of new skills; they foster teamwork and stimulate creative problem-solving.

The value of conferences, meanwhile, lies in their ability to expose attendees to the cutting edge of data analytics. Here, one can glean insights from industry leaders, network with peers, and discover emerging trends. Leaders should not only encourage attendance but facilitate it – be it through funding or flexible scheduling.

Access to learning resources – online courses, webinars, books, and journals – is equally crucial. In an age where knowledge is power, ensuring that team members have unfettered access to these resources is paramount. Leaders can take this a step further by fostering a culture of knowledge sharing, where learning becomes a collective endeavor.

Why, one might ask, is all this effort necessary? The answer is simple yet profound: the landscape of data analytics is in constant flux. What is cutting-edge today might be obsolete

LEADERSHIP IN THE AGE OF DATA: HARNESSING INFORMATION FOR STRATEGIC ADVANTAGE

tomorrow. Continuous learning is not just beneficial; it is essential for maintaining a competitive edge.

One cannot overemphasize the importance of creating a culture that celebrates curiosity and rewards initiative. Encourage your team to ask questions, to seek out new learning opportunities, and to challenge the status quo.

A single sentence stands out in this discourse: Knowledge is the currency of the future.

Leaders must not only preach the gospel of continuous learning but practice it. By embodying the principles of growth and development, leaders set a powerful example for their teams. This is leadership in the age of data – not just directing, but inspiring, not just managing, but growing alongside your team.

Consider the story of a leader who, despite her busy schedule, dedicates time each week to learn a new data visualization tool. Her commitment inspires her team, leading to a wave of self-initiated learning across the group. This story illustrates that leadership is as much about what you do as what you say.

Quoting the renowned educator John Dewey, "Education is not preparation for life; education is life itself." This rings especially true in the context of data analytics. The pursuit of knowledge must be ceaseless, for in this pursuit lies the key to innovation, excellence, and ultimately, strategic advantage.

Leaders, therefore, must not only provide the tools for learning but also create an environment where growth is part of the

DNA. This involves recognizing and rewarding progress, setting clear development goals, and encouraging a mindset where every challenge is seen as a learning opportunity.

In conclusion, leading in the age of data demands more than just technical savvy or managerial competence. It calls for a commitment to fostering an environment where continuous learning and professional growth are woven into the very fabric of your team's culture. This chapter has explored the pathways to achieving this – through training programs, workshops, conferences, and access to learning resources. But beyond these tangible tools, it is the intangible qualities of curiosity, perseverance, and a willingness to grow that will truly define leadership in this new era.

As we forge ahead, let us carry with us the conviction that our greatest asset in the age of data is not the information we possess but our ability to learn, adapt, and grow. This is the hallmark of true leadership, and the key to harnessing information for strategic advantage.

Empowering Teams With Data Literacy and Tools

In a digital age where data reigns supreme, the true power lies not in the sheer volume of information available but in our capacity to harness it for strategic advantage. This reality begets a critical question: How can leaders empower their teams to effectively navigate this vast sea of data? The answer lies in enhancing data literacy and ensuring access to the necessary tools and technologies.

LEADERSHIP IN THE AGE OF DATA: HARNESSING INFORMATION FOR STRATEGIC ADVANTAGE

Embarking on this journey requires a clear understanding of what data literacy entails. It is the ability to read, understand, create, and communicate data as information. Much like literacy in the traditional sense, which empowers individuals to decipher written words, data literacy equips team members with the skills to make informed decisions based on data analysis and interpretation.

Imagine a team where every member, irrespective of their role, possesses the foundational skills to interpret data charts, question the reliability of data sources, and make predictions based on data trends. Such a team is not a distant dream but an attainable reality, provided leaders are committed to fostering these skills.

Why, then, is data literacy so crucial? The answer is multifaceted. In an environment inundated with data, the ability to sift through noise to find relevant insights is invaluable. It transforms data from a potential source of overwhelm to a strategic asset. Moreover, when team members are data literate, they can contribute more effectively to the organization's data-driven goals, ensuring that decisions are made on a solid evidence base rather than gut feeling or intuition.

But data literacy alone is not enough. Teams also need access to the right tools and technologies to analyze, visualize, and interpret data. From sophisticated data analytics software to simple visualization tools, the technology landscape offers a plethora of options. Leaders play a pivotal role in selecting and providing access to these tools, ensuring they align with the team's needs and the organization's objectives.

Consider the story of a marketing team equipped with a powerful data analytics tool tailored to their specific needs. With this tool, they can track customer engagement across multiple platforms in real time, enabling them to tailor their campaigns with unprecedented precision. The result? A significant uptick in customer engagement and a notable boost in ROI. This scenario underscores the transformative impact of marrying data literacy with the right technologies.

How, then, can leaders ensure their teams are both data literate and well-equipped with the necessary tools? The roadmap is threefold: education, access, and culture.

Education involves providing ongoing training and learning opportunities to build and refine data literacy skills. This might include workshops, online courses, and even informal learning sessions where team members can share insights and learn from one another.

Access goes beyond merely purchasing software. It means ensuring that team members have the necessary hardware, adequate training on how to use the tools, and ongoing support to troubleshoot issues and explore advanced features.

Culture, perhaps the most critical element, involves creating an environment where data-driven decision-making is the norm, curiosity is encouraged, and failures are viewed as learning opportunities. In such a culture, team members feel

LEADERSHIP IN THE AGE OF DATA: HARNESSING INFORMATION FOR STRATEGIC ADVANTAGE

empowered to experiment with data, ask questions, and seek out new tools and technologies that can enhance their work.

A poignant question arises: Are leaders ready to embark on this journey? The path to empowering teams with data literacy and tools is not without its challenges. It requires a commitment of time, resources, and, most importantly, a willingness to lead by example.

In an organization where leaders champion the use of data, celebrate the wins derived from data-driven insights, and openly discuss the lessons learned from data-related missteps, a powerful message is sent. It signals to the team that data literacy and the use of analytical tools are not just organizational priorities but are valued and expected competencies.

The journey toward data empowerment is an ongoing one, marked by continuous learning and adaptation. As leaders, our role is to pave the way, removing barriers and providing the support our teams need to thrive in this data-centric world.

In conclusion, the age of data presents an unprecedented opportunity for strategic advantage. But harnessing this potential requires more than access to data; it demands a workforce that is literate in data and equipped with the right tools. As leaders, we have the privilege and responsibility to empower our teams in this endeavor. The future belongs to those who understand that in the realm of data, knowledge is power, but the ability to apply that knowledge is even more powerful.

Emerging Trends and Future Considerations

Emerging Technologies and Their Impact (AI, ML, IoT)

In the swirling maelstrom of the digital age, a trio of technologies stands out, poised to reshape the very fabric of leadership and strategy: Artificial Intelligence (AI), Machine Learning (ML), and the Internet of Things (IoT). These are not mere tools in the hands of the adept; they are the vanguards of a revolution, transforming data into a wellspring of strategic advantage.

At the heart of this transformation lies AI, a technology that mimics the decision-making capabilities of the human mind. Imagine a world where predictive analytics not only forecasts trends but also uncovers hidden correlations, weaving together disparate data threads into a tapestry of insight. AI does not tire. It does not falter in its task, processing vast oceans of data with unfathomable speed and accuracy. But what does this mean for leadership?

Leaders equipped with AI can make informed decisions with a clarity once deemed impossible. They navigate through uncertainty with the confidence of data-driven insights, charting courses that would have remained obscured in the fog of complexity. Picture a CEO assessing market dynamics, where AI illuminates the path to innovation, revealing opportunities veiled to the human eye.

LEADERSHIP IN THE AGE OF DATA: HARNESSING INFORMATION FOR STRATEGIC ADVANTAGE

Machine Learning, AI's close kin, takes this a step further. It learns. Through exposure to data, ML algorithms improve, adapt, and evolve. They transform raw data into a learning journey, where each piece of information is a stepping stone to deeper understanding. This continuous cycle of learning and adaptation is pivotal. It means systems can predict customer behavior with uncanny accuracy, optimize operations in real-time, and even preempt disruptions before they ripple through the market.

Consider the impact on supply chain management. An ML algorithm, fed with historical data and real-time inputs, can predict supply chain disruptions before they happen. It can suggest alternative suppliers, optimize routes, and even adjust production schedules on the fly. The result? A resilient, agile supply chain that can weather the storms of uncertainty.

Then there's the Internet of Things (IoT), a network of interconnected devices that communicate, collect, and exchange data. These devices, embedded in the everyday, offer a granular view of the world that was previously invisible. From sensors in manufacturing equipment to wearables monitoring health metrics, the IoT transforms the physical world into a domain of data.

The implications for leadership are profound. With IoT, leaders gain visibility into every corner of their operations. They can monitor performance in real-time, anticipate failures before they occur, and even tailor experiences to individual preferences. The IoT blurs the lines between the digital and the physical, opening new avenues for innovation and engagement.

But what does this mean for the future? How will these technologies reshape the landscape of leadership and strategy?

The opportunities are as vast as they are varied. Data analytics, powered by AI and ML, can uncover new market opportunities, streamline operations, and enhance customer experiences. Automation, fueled by the same technologies, can free humans from mundane tasks, allowing them to focus on creative and strategic endeavors.

Perhaps more intriguingly, these technologies pave the way for new business models. Consider the potential of a service model that leverages AI to offer personalized recommendations, or an IoT-driven approach that transforms product usage data into insights for continuous improvement.

Yet, with great power comes great responsibility. Leaders must navigate the ethical considerations of data privacy, the risks of over-reliance on technology, and the challenge of ensuring these benefits are equitably distributed.

So, what's the verdict? Are we ready to embrace this revolution?

As we stand on the brink of this new era, one thing is clear: the future belongs to those who can harness these technologies, not as mere tools, but as allies in the quest for strategic advantage. It demands a new breed of leader, one who views data not as a resource to be exploited, but as a compass guiding the way to innovation, resilience, and unparalleled competitive edge.

The dawn of leadership in the age of data is upon us. Will you seize the moment?

Preparing for the Future: Skills and Capabilities for Next-Gen Leaders

In the sweeping vistas of the future, where the digital and physical realms intertwine with the elegance of a symphony, leaders stand at the helm of an unprecedented transformation. Gone are the days when decisions were made in the solitude of a boardroom, guided solely by intuition and experience. In this new era, a confluence of data and technology demands a reimagining of leadership—a paradigm shift towards skills and capabilities that resonate with the rhythm of innovation and change.

Imagine a world that changes with the swiftness of the wind. Here, adaptability isn't just a trait; it's the very foundation upon which the future of leadership is built. Leaders must be as fluid as the data streams that inform their decisions, capable of navigating the twists and turns of the market with grace and agility. They are the reeds that bend in the storm but never break, transforming challenges into opportunities with a blend of creativity and resilience.

In the vast ocean of the digital age, technological literacy is the compass that guides leaders. It's not merely about understanding the latest gadgets and gizmos but grasping the profound impact of technology on business, society, and the environment. Leaders must dive deep into the digital seas, exploring the potential of AI, ML, and IoT to drive innovation, efficiency, and sustainability. They must also be vigilant, ensuring that their voyage respects the boundaries of ethics and privacy, steering clear of the treacherous waters of misuse and overreliance.

With the horizon constantly shifting, strategic foresight becomes an invaluable skill for leaders. It's the ability to gaze into the future, to discern patterns in the chaos of data, and to envision pathways that lead to success. This is not about predicting the future with absolute certainty—a feat not even the most advanced AI can achieve—but about preparing for it with a mindset that embraces change, values flexibility, and understands the power of informed speculation. Leaders with strategic foresight are the architects of the future, crafting strategies that are as dynamic as the world around them.

Amidst the whirlwind of progress, ethical considerations remain the steadfast compass that guides leaders. In a world awash with data, the line between innovation and intrusion can blur, making it imperative for leaders to anchor their actions in a strong ethical framework. They must navigate the delicate balance between leveraging data for strategic advantage and respecting the privacy and rights of individuals. Ethical leaders are the beacon of trust and integrity, illuminating the path for others to follow.

In the crucible of the modern world, leadership is continuously forged and re-forged. It demands a holistic approach, one that combines adaptability, technological literacy, strategic foresight, and ethical considerations into a cohesive whole. Leaders who embody these qualities are not just prepared for the future; they are actively shaping it, molding the raw potential of data and technology into a legacy of innovation and progress.

As we stand on the threshold of a new era, one question echoes through the corridors of time and space: Are you ready to be a leader in the age of data?

The future awaits your answer.

Ethical AI and Its Implications for Leadership

In the labyrinth of the digital age, where information cascades like a relentless river, the emergence of Artificial Intelligence (AI) stands as a beacon of potential and peril. It is a tool that, when wielded with wisdom, can carve pathways to unprecedented strategic advantages. Yet, in the hands of those who overlook its ethical implications, it can morph into a double-edged sword, cutting through the fabric of trust and fairness with startling ease. This chapter delves into the ethical quagmire surrounding AI in decision-making, unraveling the complexities of bias, transparency, and accountability. It seeks to offer leaders a compass to navigate these murky waters, ensuring their journey towards harnessing AI aligns with the highest ethical standards, nurturing an environment of fairness and trust.

Imagine a world where decisions are not just informed by AI but are made by it. Here, bias lurks in the shadows, a silent specter born from the very data that feeds these intelligent systems. Bias in AI is not merely an error in coding; it is a reflection of our societal prejudices, a mirror revealing the skewed perspectives that permeate our information sources. The question then arises: How can leaders ensure that their AI tools do not perpetuate or, worse, amplify these biases?

Transparency becomes the sword to cut through this Gordian knot. Leaders must demand and foster transparency in the development and deployment of AI systems. This begins with an open dialogue about the sources of data, the assumptions embedded within algorithms, and the potential for biased outcomes. By shedding light on these processes, leaders can identify and mitigate biases, ensuring that AI serves as a tool for equity, not inequality.

With the power of AI comes a veil of complexity, obscuring the inner workings of algorithms from those they impact. This opacity challenges the very foundations of trust, leaving stakeholders questioning the validity and fairness of decisions. How, then, can leaders lift this veil, making AI's decision-making processes transparent and comprehensible?

The answer lies in the commitment to explainability. Leaders must prioritize the development and use of AI systems that not only make decisions but can also explain them in terms understandable to humans. This commitment to explainability empowers stakeholders, enabling them to grasp the rationale behind AI-driven decisions, fostering an atmosphere of trust and accountability.

LEADERSHIP IN THE AGE OF DATA: HARNESSING INFORMATION FOR STRATEGIC ADVANTAGE

Responsibility looms large in the age of AI. As leaders integrate AI into their decision-making processes, the question of accountability becomes paramount. When an AI system makes a decision that has negative consequences, who is to be held accountable? The developers of the AI? The leaders who implemented it? The data that trained it?

Leaders must embrace the mantle of accountability, ensuring that mechanisms are in place to evaluate and respond to the outcomes of AI decisions. This involves not just a reactive stance, ready to address issues as they arise, but a proactive approach that anticipates potential pitfalls and institutes safeguards against them. Accountability in AI is not a burden to be shirked but a cornerstone of ethical leadership, reinforcing the trust of those who are affected by AI's decisions.

In the wilderness of the digital age, ethical leadership is the compass that guides us. Leaders must become stewards of AI, championing its ethical use to ensure it acts as a force for good. This entails a commitment to continuous learning, staying abreast of the evolving landscape of AI technology and its ethical implications. Leaders must also foster an environment of ethical vigilance, encouraging teams to question and critique, ensuring that ethical considerations are at the forefront of AI initiatives.

Moreover, collaboration emerges as a vital tool in this journey. By engaging with ethicists, technologists, and the wider community, leaders can gain diverse perspectives, enriching their understanding and application of ethical AI. Through dialogue and partnership, leaders can navigate the ethical complexities of AI, charting a course that leverages its power for the strategic advantage without sacrificing the values of fairness and trust.

In conclusion, the dawn of AI in leadership heralds both opportunities and challenges. As we venture further into this uncharted territory, the principles of bias mitigation, transparency, accountability, and ethical stewardship must light the way. Leaders who embrace these principles will not only harness the strategic advantages of AI but will also build a legacy of integrity and trust.

Are you prepared to lead with ethical courage in the age of AI? The future is watching, and it demands an answer steeped in ethical conviction and action.

Staying Ahead of the Curve: Continuous Learning and Adaptation

In a world where data streams flow unceasingly, carving the landscape of our professional and personal lives, leaders find themselves at a crossroads. The age of data, with its vast reservoirs of information and rapid technological advancements, demands a new kind of leadership. A leadership that is not only informed by the present but is also perpetually learning, adapting, and preparing for the uncharted terrains of the future. This chapter, "Staying Ahead of the Curve: Continuous Learning and Adaptation," explores the quintessential strategies that leaders must embrace to harness information for strategic advantage in this dynamic era.

LEADERSHIP IN THE AGE OF DATA: HARNESSING INFORMATION FOR STRATEGIC ADVANTAGE

The journey through the digital age is akin to navigating the high seas. Just as the mariner must read the stars, understand the winds, and adapt to the ever-changing elements, so too must leaders in the age of data be adept at interpreting the vast skies of information, discerning the prevailing technological winds, and adjusting their sails to catch the gusts of innovation. But how does one cultivate such adaptability and foresight?

Firstly, it is imperative to cultivate a culture of continuous learning within oneself and one's organization. The landscape of data and technology evolves at an astonishing pace, rendering yesterday's cutting-edge knowledge obsolete. Leaders must foster an environment where learning is not a one-time event but a continuous journey. Encourage your teams to explore, experiment, and educate themselves on the latest trends in data analytics, machine learning, and other relevant fields. Remember, a leader's hunger for knowledge is contagious, spreading throughout the organization, inspiring all to climb higher.

How do you stay informed about the latest trends? Regularly immerse yourself in the sea of knowledge available through reputable tech blogs, journals, and forums. Attend industry conferences, not just as a participant, but as an active networker and learner. Engage with thought leaders and innovators, absorbing their insights and perspectives. Through these interactions, you will not only stay abreast of emerging technologies but also gain foresight into how they might impact your industry and organization.

Visualization is key. Imagine a future where your organization not only leverages the current state-of-the-art in data analytics but leads the charge in implementing next-generation technologies. What does this future look like? How did you navigate the challenges and opportunities along the way? By vividly picturing this future, you set a strategic direction, motivating yourself and your team to acquire the knowledge and skills necessary to turn this vision into reality.

Adaptation, the twin pillar of continuous learning, demands flexibility and willingness to pivot when necessary. In the realm of data and technology, what works today may not suffice tomorrow. Leaders must, therefore, cultivate an adaptive mindset, one that is open to experimentation and unafraid of failure. Foster an organizational culture where failure is not a setback but a stepping stone to innovation. Encourage your teams to experiment with new data analytics tools and methodologies, learning from each attempt and continuously refining their approach.

Have you ever considered the power of cross-disciplinary learning? Often, breakthroughs in one field can inform and inspire innovations in another. By encouraging your team to draw connections between seemingly disparate fields, you unlock a wellspring of creative solutions. For instance, insights from behavioral economics can enhance customer data analysis, leading to more effective marketing strategies.

In the pursuit of staying ahead of the curve, never underestimate the power of mentorship and collaboration. Pairing seasoned professionals with younger team members

LEADERSHIP IN THE AGE OF DATA: HARNESSING INFORMATION FOR STRATEGIC ADVANTAGE

not only facilitates the transfer of knowledge but also fosters a culture of mutual learning and innovation. Similarly, collaborations with external partners, such as academic institutions and other organizations, can provide fresh perspectives and access to cutting-edge research.

In conclusion, the leaders who will thrive in the age of data are those who view continuous learning and adaptation not as tasks to be checked off but as fundamental principles to be woven into the fabric of their leadership style. Such leaders do not merely react to the waves of change; they anticipate them, navigate through them, and emerge at the forefront of innovation.

Are you ready to embark on this journey of continuous learning and adaptation? The path is challenging, no doubt, but the rewards—strategic advantage, innovation, and leadership excellence—are well worth the effort. Let us set sail into the future, armed with knowledge, adaptability, and the unwavering resolve to lead our organizations to new horizons.

Remember, the age of data is not just about technology; it's about the vision, strategy, and leadership that harness technology for the greater good. As we voyage through this age, let our guiding stars be continuous learning and adaptation, illuminating the path to strategic advantage and success.

Best Practices for Data-Driven Leadership

Lessons Learned From Real-World Case Studies

In the fast-paced world of modern business, data stands as the new currency. Through the annals of this book, we have traversed the landscapes of numerous case studies, each a testament to the power of data when harnessed with precision and strategic insight. Now, as we stand on the brink of concluding our journey, it's time to distill the essence of these narratives into tangible lessons for leaders aiming to navigate the treacherous waters of the data age.

Undoubtedly, the first and most profound lesson emerges from the tale of a small online retailer that, against all odds, transformed itself into a market leader. Remember the story of "EcoWear," a startup that leveraged consumer behavior data to tailor its marketing strategies? From this narrative, the importance of listening to the data sings clear. It's not just about collecting vast amounts of information but about interpreting it, understanding the story it tells, and acting upon it. EcoWear's success was not a stroke of luck but a result of meticulous data analysis, leading to actionable insights. The takeaway? Data-driven decision-making is not a luxury but a necessity.

Venture next into the saga of "HealthTrack," a healthcare provider that utilized predictive analytics to improve patient

LEADERSHIP IN THE AGE OF DATA: HARNESSING INFORMATION FOR STRATEGIC ADVANTAGE

outcomes. Here, the power of predictive data shone brightly, showcasing its ability to not only react to current trends but also anticipate future ones. HealthTrack's approach to integrating data analytics into patient care significantly reduced readmission rates and improved overall health outcomes. This case study reinforces the lesson that in the hands of visionary leaders, data can be a tool not just for business efficiency, but for making a profound impact on human lives.

What about the story of "GreenTech Innovations," a company that stood at the forefront of the green technology revolution? Their strategic use of data to optimize supply chain operations and reduce waste serves as a beacon for sustainability efforts worldwide. GreenTech's journey underscores the lesson that data is not just a tool for profit maximization but can be a catalyst for positive environmental change. It shows leaders the importance of aligning data strategies with broader societal values.

Each of these case studies brings to light the critical role of agility in today's data-driven landscape. Consider how "FinTech Global," a financial technology startup, harnessed real-time data to adapt swiftly to market changes. This agility allowed them to outmaneuver larger, more established competitors. Thus, the lesson is clear: in the age of data, adaptability is key. The ability to pivot based on data-driven insights can be the difference between leading the market and lagging behind.

But how can leaders cultivate these capabilities within their organizations? It begins with fostering a culture that values data literacy at all levels. Encouraging curiosity, promoting continuous learning, and providing teams with the tools they need to analyze and interpret data are foundational steps. Moreover, leaders must champion the cause of data ethics, ensuring that the pursuit of data-driven advantage does not come at the cost of privacy or integrity.

Imagine a future where every decision, from the minutiae of daily operations to the grand strategies that define a company's path, is informed by data. This vision is not just a distant dream but a tangible reality for those willing to embrace the lessons from our case studies.

So, what does it take to lead in the age of data? It requires a blend of courage and curiosity, the boldness to question conventional wisdom, and the humility to learn from what the data reveals.

As you, the reader, stand at the crossroads of knowledge and action, ask yourself: How can I apply these lessons in my own organization? What steps can I take to harness the transformative power of data?

Remember, the journey does not end here. The age of data is ever-evolving, and with it, the strategies for leveraging information for strategic advantage. Stay curious, stay informed, and above all, stay committed to the path of data-driven leadership.

LEADERSHIP IN THE AGE OF DATA: HARNESSING INFORMATION FOR STRATEGIC ADVANTAGE

In the final analysis, the real-world case studies presented in this book are more than just stories. They are a call to action—a beacon for leaders navigating the complex, data-driven landscapes of the modern world.

Embrace the power of data. Let it be your guide to strategic advantage in an age where information is the ultimate tool for leadership.

Recommendations for Successful Data-Driven Transformation

In the wake of these compelling narratives, the path forward becomes illuminated, guiding leaders toward the successful implementation of a data-driven transformation within their organizations. This journey, while filled with potential, requires a deliberate approach, keen insight, and unwavering dedication. The following recommendations serve as a beacon for those ready to harness the power of data for strategic advantage.

At the heart of any successful transformation lies the culture of the organization. How can you, as a leader, instill a culture that not only values but thrives on data?

First, lead by example. Demonstrate a commitment to data-driven decision-making in your actions and communications. When the leadership team visibly relies on data for critical decisions, it sets a tone that resonates throughout the organization.

Second, remove the stigma from failure. Encourage experimentation and learning from data-driven initiatives, even when they don't yield the expected outcomes. Such an environment fosters innovation and continuous improvement.

Finally, recognize and reward data-driven achievements. Whether it's through formal awards or simple acknowledgments in team meetings, celebrating successes reinforces the value placed on data-driven efforts.

A common pitfall for organizations embarking on a data journey is the misalignment of data strategies with overarching business objectives. How can this alignment be ensured?

Begin by clearly defining your business goals. These should be specific, measurable, achievable, relevant, and time-bound (SMART). With these goals in hand, develop a data strategy that directly supports them. For instance, if a goal is to improve customer satisfaction by 20% within a year, your data strategy might focus on collecting and analyzing customer feedback data to identify improvement areas.

Next, involve stakeholders from across the organization in the development of the data strategy. This collaborative approach ensures that the strategy is comprehensive and considers the diverse needs of different departments.

Innovation is not a one-time event but a continuous process. How can leaders cultivate an environment where innovation and continuous improvement are part of the DNA?

LEADERSHIP IN THE AGE OF DATA: HARNESSING INFORMATION FOR STRATEGIC ADVANTAGE

Encourage cross-functional teams to tackle complex problems. These teams bring diverse perspectives and can leverage data in novel ways to find solutions.

Invest in training and tools that empower employees to analyze and interpret data effectively. A workforce skilled in data literacy is more likely to innovate and identify opportunities for improvement.

Regularly review and adjust your data strategy. The business environment is dynamic, and what worked yesterday may not work tomorrow. Be prepared to pivot based on new data insights and market conditions.

In the pursuit of a data-driven advantage, never lose sight of the ethical implications. How can leaders ensure that their data practices uphold the highest standards of integrity and ethics?

First, establish clear policies regarding data privacy and security. These should comply with all relevant laws and regulations, but they should also reflect your organization's commitment to ethical standards.

Second, be transparent about data collection and usage practices. Customers and employees alike should understand what data is being collected, why it's being collected, and how it will be used.

Lastly, create a culture of accountability. When everyone in the organization feels responsible for upholding ethical data practices, it becomes a collective effort that strengthens trust and integrity.

Imagine a future where every decision made within your organization is informed by data. This future is not only possible but within reach for those who embrace the recommendations outlined above.

Building a data-driven culture, aligning data strategy with business goals, fostering innovation and continuous improvement, and embracing ethical data practices are not mere suggestions but essential components of successful data-driven transformation.

Let these recommendations guide you as you navigate the complexities of the data age. Remember, the journey toward data-driven leadership is ongoing, filled with challenges and opportunities alike. But for those who persist, the rewards are substantial.

So, as you close this chapter, reflect on the path that lies ahead. How will you apply these recommendations in your organization? What steps will you take today to ensure a successful data-driven transformation tomorrow?

The age of data awaits. Embrace its challenges, harness its power, and lead your organization to new heights of strategic advantage.

Call to Action: Embracing the Data Revolution for Leadership Success

As we stand on the cusp of a new era, the data revolution beckons with open arms, promising a future where informed decisions lead the way to unprecedented success and

LEADERSHIP IN THE AGE OF DATA: HARNESSING INFORMATION FOR STRATEGIC ADVANTAGE

innovation. This final chapter is not merely a conclusion but a clarion call to action for leaders everywhere. Embrace the data revolution fully and take your rightful place at the forefront of this transformative movement.

Why, you might ask, is this step so crucial? The answer lies not in the data itself but in what it represents: knowledge, insight, and the key to unlocking potentials previously untapped. Imagine navigating a ship in the vast ocean without a compass or a map. Such has been the journey of decision-making without data. But now, equipped with the right tools and strategies, you can chart a course through the most turbulent waters with confidence and precision.

Leadership in the age of data is not about possession but about application. It's one thing to have access to data; it's another entirely to harness it for strategic advantage. This distinction is crucial. Data-driven leadership transcends traditional boundaries, enabling you to anticipate trends, address challenges proactively, and seize opportunities that others may not even see.

But how, exactly, can you embrace this revolution? Start by fostering a culture of curiosity and learning within your organization. Encourage your team to ask questions, to delve deeper into the 'why' and 'how' of every situation. Through this lens, every challenge becomes an opportunity to learn and grow.

Invest in technology and training that empower your team to make the most of the data at their disposal. Tools and platforms evolve, but the ability to think critically and analytically is timeless. Equip your team with these skills, and watch as they transform challenges into stepping stones for success.

Moreover, collaboration across departments and disciplines can unearth insights that might otherwise remain hidden. Encourage open dialogue and sharing of information. The synergy between different areas of expertise can lead to breakthroughs that propel your organization forward in the data age.

Remember, data is not just numbers and charts; it's the voice of your customers, the rhythm of the market, the pulse of your organization. Listening to these signals and understanding their message is the essence of data-driven leadership.

Are you ready to take the bold step into this new age? Are you prepared to lead with insight, agility, and foresight?

The journey ahead is as exciting as it is daunting. The path may not always be clear, and challenges will undoubtedly arise. But with a steadfast commitment to embracing the data revolution, you will navigate this landscape with the acumen and precision of a seasoned explorer.

Imagine the possibilities that lie ahead. A future where every decision, big or small, is informed by data. Where your organization not only adapts to change but anticipates and shapes it. This is the promise of data-driven leadership, and it is within your grasp.

LEADERSHIP IN THE AGE OF DATA: HARNESSING INFORMATION FOR STRATEGIC ADVANTAGE

So, as we turn the page on this chapter, let it not be the end but the beginning of your journey. A journey marked by innovation, growth, and transformation. The data revolution is not a fleeting trend; it is the future of leadership.

The question now is not if you will embrace this revolution, but how. How will you leverage the power of data to lead your organization into a new era of success? The tools, strategies, and insights shared in this book are your compass. Use them to navigate the complexities of the data age, to empower your team, and to lead with confidence.

The age of data awaits. Embrace its challenges, harness its power, and lead your organization to new heights of strategic advantage.

Let this be your call to action. Rise to the occasion. Embrace the data revolution with open arms and lead your organization toward a future brimming with potential and promise.

The time to act is now.

About the Author

Ikwe Gideon stands at the forefront of data analytics and technology, backed by an impressive academic and professional background. With degrees in Data Science and Analytics and Mathematics/Statistics from Cardiff University, along with certifications like Microsoft Certified: Power BI Data Analyst Associate and Azure Fundamentals, Gideon combines deep theoretical knowledge with practical expertise. His career, spanning over two decades, has seen impactful work across sectors like retail, technology, and telecommunications, where he's utilized data to drive strategic growth and efficiency. Gideon excels in business intelligence, data analytics, and risk management, armed with skills in Azure Cloud, SQL, Power BI, and a strong grasp of data governance and ethics.

A seasoned leader, Gideon has spearheaded complex projects, leveraging tools like Jira and Azure DevOps for optimal execution. His work in BI strategy, revenue assurance, and fraud detection at companies like Shop City Marketplace

Limited, Mozambique Cellular, Mobile Communication Company, Iran (MCCI), and Airtel Africa has significantly improved their data analytics strategy, data governance, and financial health.

As an Amazon author, Gideon shares his extensive knowledge on data-driven decision-making, analytics, and the ethical use of technology in business, positioning himself as a thought leader in analytics. His dedication to innovation and excellence in his writing aims to equip professionals with the insights needed to leverage analytics for strategic advantage, making his books essential for navigating the data-rich business landscape.

www.ingramcontent.com/pod-product-compliance
Lightning Source LLC
Chambersburg PA
CBHW052210220526
45471CB00004B/1900